Behold, Come See Who He Is

Finding God In Everyday Places

Lauretta Phillips

ISBN – 13:978-1-7216-2348-8

ISBN – 10:1-721-623-485

Behold, Come See Who He Is

Finding God In Everyday Places

By Lauretta Phillips

Contents

Dedication

This book is dedicated to all those who shared their stories with me, to those whom I asked and those whom I didn't. They are the ones who see God in everyday living. I want to thank them. I also want to thank those who have helped to produce this book in so many ways. Here are just a few.

Lorna MacDonald Czarnota who is my accountability partner and keeps me going when it is so easy to be distracted by everyday living. Lorna also contributed the story about grief.

Anne-Marie Forer who is the best editor a friend could have. She worked tirelessly with me to make sure this book was as good as it could be. We spent hours on the phone and through email talking and changing and re writing. We shared a beautiful retreat space together and although the woods and the water were calling to us, we still found time to do the corrections line by line. She is dedicated and honest and she helps me see what I wrote the way a reader would.

Sisters Cora Ciampi and Carol Nichols who encouraged me to continue to write just because. They are both talented authors and true sisters. Cora has also contributed a story here.

Lesa Ann Stoddard who helped create the story. The best daughter a mother could have.

All those friends and sisters in Christ who seemed to love to read what I put down on these pages and kept on asking, "How is your new book coming?"

But most of all to the God who gave me the strength and power and gift of words to make this book what it is. May the words of my mouth and the meditation of my heart be acceptable to you o' my God. My redeemer.

Preface

Behold, Come See Who He Is.

Finding God in Everyday Places

I finished my first nonfiction book and took a breather to work on other things and do some marketing for my storytelling business. It was good to have a break and I found myself getting more and more involved in The Franklin Studio which is a coffee house and craft studio in Franklin New Hampshire that sells all New Hampshire made quality crafts and artisan pieces. I was volunteering two and sometimes three days a week and sewing quilted things to sell there. I love to create and creating beautiful things from fabric is a joy.

On April 2, 2016, I held my book release party at The Franklin Studio and it was a huge success. A Closer Walk – One Woman's Journey sold well and continues to sell. It will probably continue to sell for many years to come. It is a "God thing".

 I have been writing every day. Some of my stories are fiction, some nonfiction, but since the book release all have been short pieces, nothing as long or defined as a book.

I read over my journals every once in a while to get a feel of where I have come from and how I am growing. While reading the most recent ones, it struck me that a lot of these entries had a central theme. Many journal entries were actual stories of people and things in my life that let God shine through.   I was finding God in everyday places and everyday people. I had learned to look for Him. One day as I was in my early morning meditation, it came to me that I should put together the stories that followed this theme. Maybe I could help others to see God in everyday life if I could show them ways to find Him through stories. Perhaps it might help if I could show them where to look and how to see Him.

As with the last book, I procrastinated about it. When God asks you to do something, however, you probably should listen. Revelation 3:10 says "I chastise and discipline those I love, so do my will with zest and zeal." If I want to have God's best for my life, I should give Him my best. That is what led to the writing of this book of stories that God put on my heart to share with you.

The people who blessed me with their stories have given me permission to share them with you. Some of them have asked to be anonymous and I have changed their names or left names out to accommodate their wishes. The others have written their stories for me to share or dictated them to me. I hope you will enjoy these stories and share them with others. I know you are going to be blessed by these stories and will see God in them too.

Chapter One

Turn Your Eyes Upon Jesus

Turn your eyes upon Jesus,

Look full in His wonderful face

And the things of Earth will grow strangely dim

In the light of His glory and grace.

These are some of the words to an old song I learned as a child. This is one of the songs that my mother sang and taught us to sing. This song was written by Helen H. Lemmel (1863-1961) in 1922. She was a gifted singer and songwriter who wrote over 500 songs. This one is by far the most popular. It was inspired by a tract written by missionary Isabella Lilias titled <u>Focused</u>.

It has taken many years for me to learn to see Jesus in everyday life. It is not hard to see Him in church or in a group of church people. At least it shouldn't be. It is more difficult to see Him in the everyday living on this earth that we all do.

When I ask to see God in everyday life, I just have to be mindful of Him. Where would He be? How would He look? What would He be doing? Who would He be with?

It is easy to see Him in the early morning sunrise or in the singing of the first birds. It is easy to see

9

Him in the little child who instinctively reaches out to help another little child. It is easy to see Him in the ones you love.

But where do you find Him in the hospital waiting room or the doctor's office? What about the disagreement you had with your spouse or partner or the weather disaster that happened to destroy whole towns? Where do you see Him then? Where is He in the tears of heartbreak or the side of a grave? He is there. How do you see Him when you are working and no one seems to notice the hard work you do?

How do you see Him when the people around you are complaining about the boss and the regulations of a company?   He is there. Can you find Him in the tears as well as the laughter? Yes, you just have to be willing to notice. You just have to be open to seeing Him.   Ephesians 1:18 (NAS) says "Open the eyes of my heart Lord, I want to see you."

Two of the things I pray about each day are these. "Father let me see how I can be a blessing to someone today and open my eyes to see you."

John 16:24 says ask and you will receive, so that your joy may be made full. (NAS)

Whenever I ask whom I can bless that day there are always a few who come to mind. I often won't even be out of the house before I have some contact with someone who needs blessings of some kind.

You, too, may find many ways to bless someone each day. Someone calls to ask for prayer for a loved one. Another will want to meet for lunch or coffee, just to talk. A neighbor lady will be having an especially lonely day. You can see someone in need on the street or in the store. It doesn't take a fortune to help others. It only costs a stamp to send a note to someone to cheer them. Phone calls are easy to make and can last for only as long as you have the time. Even a Facebook or email message is easy to do and takes almost no time. There is always a way.

I can do much with what I have. It isn't hard to drive a couple blocks further so I can wave at the old woman in her kitchen window every morning. I know she waits for me because she waves her plastic flowers at me to let me know she is up and about.

It might be a nuisance, but it isn't hard to wait while a grandchild watches the ants going in and out of the doorway to their house. He is amazed at how busy they all are. He wants to know all about them and what they are doing. It is easy to see God's blessings when you are watching ants and talking with a child.

But what about the other part of my prayer? How do I see God in everyday life? I sometimes find Him in the most unusual places. Like when Jesus finds Zacchaeus high in a tree and goes home with

11

him to dinner, I find Him in places I've never thought to look before. I find Him in the eyes of a child or the smile of the store clerk's face. He's in the tilted head of a tiny flower or a huge cloud floating high above the earth. He's in the test of friendship or the trust of a dog. He is in everyday living. Some of these stories in this book are funny or happy or even joyful, but not all of them are. I guarantee, however, God is in every single one.

Prayer

"Open the eyes of our hearts Lord, we want to see you."

Scripture

Ephesians 1:18-19 (NAS)

I pray that the eyes of your heart may be enlightened, so that you will know the hope of His calling, what are the riches of the glory of His inheritance in the saints and what is the surpassing greatness of His power toward us who believe.

Question

Where do you see God?

Chapter Two

The God Lady

Christmas was coming in two short days and as usual I was shopping with my daughter and my great-grandson. He was six years old and had decided on just what he was looking for.

My daughter was off on her own doing her last-minute thing and Chris and I were headed for the sporting goods section of the store. He went straight for the fishing lures. Spotting the biggest one, he picked it up and said, "I want to get this one for Grandpa."

"Well," I said, "Grandpa doesn't go deep sea fishing and seldom fishes on any of the great lakes. This lure is for deep sea fishing. Perhaps you should choose a smaller one that he can use."

He put it back and hunted through all of them until he found the perfect one. The one that was just the right size. He said, "I am sure he does not have this one in his tackle box. I want to buy this one."

"Okay," I said "How much does it cost and do you have enough money for it?"

"Well yes, I do. I have thirty-one dollars I can spend on Christmas, but I don't have it with me. Do you have some money you can give me until we get to Grandma's?"

"Hum, let me check. Yes, I think I do but how much does that lure cost?"

It was $2.99 and he knew he had enough to buy that for sure. Then we went to the section that held plastic boxes for keeping your phone dry when you are fishing. He picked one for each of his uncles and a bigger one for his dad. Two of them were $7.99 each and the bigger one was $9.99.

He said, "Uncle Brad just needs it, but Uncle Bob rides his bike everywhere even in the rain so he really, really needs it."

I asked if his dad's phone was bigger and he said "no he needs it to keep his money dry!" The way he said it with such assurance made me laugh a bit, but he was serious. This buying presents was serious business and took a lot of thought.

We had to figure out if he had enough money to pay for these gifts. He was very relieved to know he could buy these presents. I asked him where he got so much money and he said he earned it helping Grandpa and Grandma do chores and bake cookies. He even sold some cookies at the farmers market with Grandma.

While we were walking towards the checkout with his prizes he said, "We got you a present Nana and I can tell you what it is because we are not even going to wrap it up!"

"You did? That is nice. I bet I am going to love it."

"Yep and I made it!"

"Well then, I know I am going to love it."

"Yep, I painted it and then I put these God things on it."

"Really? That's wonderful."

"Yep. That's because you're the God lady."

"Oh, why is that?"

"Because you know all about that God stuff."

He never really told me what he made because we ran into Grandma and he needed to show her his treasures.

It took me a minute to wrap my mind around what he had said. Then I thought, "If I am going to be remembered as something, being the God lady is just about the best I can think of."

On Christmas day my little guy presented me with a board about two and a half feet long by three inches tall and painted dark blue. With his Grandma's help he had placed gold decals of the nativity on it. It is a beautiful treasure I will keep standing on my bookshelf no matter what the season.

When I think back on this last Christmas season, I can't help but feel joy in the idea that somehow I am going to be remembered as a God lady. Somehow my little guy sees God in me. He hears me speak of Him and he sees the way I live and the things I do.

My little guy, like so many other little ones doesn't get to experience things about God very often. I think of all the joys he and his little friends are missing out on. The joy of seeing God in all the little things. The blessing of watching a bee or a hummingbird and knowing that God created them just as He created all things. Such complexity and simple beauty that goes hand in hand.

I only get to see him three or four times a year but we do communicate over the phone, and he writes me a letter sometimes and I write back. It is my prayer that someday he will be in the place where he can know and understand more about Jesus and His Father God. Where he can call out "Father" and know that he is heard. What a joy to see the love on his face as he talks to me, and what a blessing to see his good heart and know that somehow when we least expect it, he too will come to see and know God.

Prayer

"Father, I thank you for this precious child. I pray that he will continue to see you in me and will always call me the God lady. I pray that he too will come to you and call you Father."

Scripture

Mark 10:13-16 (NAS)

People were bringing little children to Jesus so he could lay hands on them and bless them, but the disciples rebuked them. When Jesus saw this he was indignant and said to them "Let the little children come to me and do not hinder them for the kingdom of God belongs to such as these. Truly I tell you anyone who will not receive the kingdom of heaven like a little child will never enter it." And he took the children in his arms and placed his hands on them and blessed them.

Question

Who sees God in you?

Chapter Three

In the Beginning

Spring is in the air and the turkeys are courting.
Big toms vie for the attention of a flock of about
ten females.   There are five deer that hang out in
the field beside the house morning and night.
Three of them appear to be yearlings. They kick up
their heels and bounce around like there is no
danger and they have nothing to do but to live life
to its fullest. The two mothers seem to mostly
ignore them, but they are actually on the alert for
problems. When one of them sounds the alarm,
those three youngsters pay attention and all five of
them dash off into the woods, white tails flashing.
You hardly have time to take notice before they are
gone.

Sometimes I think I know how this earth feels
when spring comes and new life abounds. There
are lambs in the barn across the road, and I noticed
the new calves in Hersey's field as I drove to town
yesterday. I like to see those new calves every
year.   It always makes me smile to know that life
continues. It does my heart good to see this
renewal of life after a period of rest. I think the
earth feels that way sometimes too.

I know Mother Earth also feels heavy-hearted with
the pollution and abuse of too many people. I try
not to be one of them. I know I do things that
contribute to the problem, things that can't be

helped because it's what we have to work with at this time.

There are other things I can do. For instance, I stopped buying plastic bottles of water unless it is absolutely necessary. Instead, I filter water at home to refill the old bottles or take a reusable cup to carry with me. I often pick up things I find on the ground. Paper, cans, plastic and food wrappers are what I find most often. Unfortunately, New Hampshire does not have a bottle return policy so cans and bottles are along the roadside where I walk.

I wasn't in the habit of picking things up, until one day while walking with a friend, I was complaining about the mess. The person I was walking with said, "We can't do anything about it. The whole world is a mess. I don't throw things on the ground so why should I pick up after the ones who do?"

I have been known to be a bit stubborn and take the opposite side of things on occasion so what she said struck a note with me. To my Pa those would have been "fightin' words."

I said, "It only took one person to throw it on the ground. It only takes one to pick it up." That day I went home with my hands and pockets full. The next time I went out walking I carried a bag and wore gloves. Who wants that stuff all over your hands anyway? You can tell the difference when I

19

don't walk that way for a while, or when I neglect to pick up the trash.

People continue to throw their trash out of their car windows or dump their bags of trash on the side of dirt roads or in wooded areas. I am not sure why. Isn't it just as easy to put it in the dumpster?

When I don't pick these things up I can almost hear my Pa saying "Hey girl, what ya doing?" Or down deep inside I think God whispers "Lauretta, don't you think you ought to take care of this earth you call home?"

I am in awe of a God who could create something as beautiful and complex as this place and I think He wants us to take care of it. It says, in Genesis 2:15 "Then the Lord God took the man and put him into the garden to cultivate it and keep it." (NAS)

Prayer

"Thank you God for letting me see the beauty you have created and help me to find the ways to help keep this earth beautiful."

Scripture

(Genesis 1:1-5 NAS)

"In the beginning God created the heavens and the earth. The earth was formless and void and darkness was over the surface of the deep, and the spirit of God was moving over the surface of the waters. Then God said 'Let there be light'

and there was light and God saw that it was good. God separated the light from the darkness. God called the light day and the darkness He called night and there was evening and there was morning, one day."

(Genesis 1:31NAS)

"And God saw all that he had made and behold it was very good."

Question

Where do you see God in nature? What can you do to help take care of this earth we call home?

Chapter Four

Redemption

One day while walking through the woods, I saw an animal crouched down beside a big oak tree. At first, I thought it was a raccoon that was trying to hide from me. As I got closer I realized it wasn't a raccoon at all but a big cat. It was huddling close to the tree but didn't seem to be aware that I was even there.

I had been told that rabies was running rampant in small animals around New Hampshire. It seems as though rabies cycles through here every few years. Last time it killed almost all the population of rabbits, raccoons, opossums and other small animals. They were just coming back and still it seemed as though they were going to be devastated again this year.

I was nervous about approaching this cat. It certainly did look sick. I considered asking my neighbor to come help me capture it in a live trap, but thought if I left it there, it would disappear. If it was rabid it would infect other animals. I was unsure what to do. Finally, I prayed, "Okay God, give me strength to help this creature if I can."

I approached it from the back and to the left of its body. It remained crouched down and huddled even closer to the tree. I could tell it was getting nervous. Without touching it, I tried to see if it was injured or had blood on it somewhere. I could not see any place that looked like an injury from the side that was exposed. I talked quietly to it and moved in a little closer. Slowly I reached out my hand and touched its back. It flinched and crouched lower to the ground but did not try to escape. That was when I realized it was dying.

I always carry a pocket knife when I am just walking in the woods and today was no exception. I squatted down closer to the animal. I took out my knife. Could I help this creature or should I put it out of its misery? Either way I could not just leave it there. I soon realized the poor creature was dying because of a collar it had outgrown. The collar seemed to be choking it to death. The cat must have escaped from someone's house and had been surviving in the woods since it was a kitten. The collar looked as though it could be embedded into the skin around the cat's neck. If it was, I would not be able to help him unless I could get the cat into a carrier and bring it to the veterinarian. That was quite unlikely as he still had enough energy for at least one last fight or flight, and I was sure he wasn't going to let me pick him up. The cat would not be here by the time I got to the cabin to pick up a pet carrier anyway.

Once again, I put my hand on its back. I held him tight to the tree and ground. The cat started to struggle as I reached out with the hand that held the knife. It looked as though the only loose spot was near the buckle right at the base of its throat. I quickly slipped the knife under that buckle and slid it to the right. It took all the strength I had to pull that knife through the collar. Thank goodness it was one of those plastic flea collars or I may not have been able to cut through it. When I did I could hear the whoosh of air as the cat began to breathe in deep raspy breaths. I could see that the collar was indeed imbedded into the skin at the back of his neck but was now apart and he could breathe. My thought was to cut away whatever part of the collar I could, but that was not to be. I wanted to pick him up, but he was just catching his breath and was not ready to be handled. Soon he pulled out of my grasp and was off down into the woods. He was gone before I could think to follow him.

For just a few minutes it seemed as though time had stopped and there was no one or nothing in the woods except that cat and his suffering. I am sure it hadn't taken long to rescue the cat. I thought about him for quite a while after that. As I walked I often looked in the woods for signs of the cat. I am sure he would have died that very day if I had not paid attention to what was going on around me. I am not sure if cats have nine lives or not. If they do, he probably had just a couple left. I would have liked to adopt him into my family and give him some love and attention, instead he ran away. I asked the neighbors to keep a sharp eye out for him, but no one ever mentioned seeing him.

The thing about the response from the cat is this, we as humans do the same thing. We ask God for His help when we are desperate, then when we have been rescued we don't wait to say thank you or to see what good things God has in store for us. We wear our scars like the cat wore the rest of the collar still attached to him instead of waiting to see if I could finish the job and help him more. I would have liked to feed him and care for him and would have given him love.

We don't let God finish the job we have asked Him to do. We take things right back into our own hands and run off into the woods without ever finding out that He not only can save us but redeem us completely. We often don't realize that if we let Him adopt us into His family, we will be His children and as such He will guide us, protect us, be with us and love us.

Prayer

"Lord help us to understand your love more clearly. Let us receive your help and your love and accept you as our Father. Bring us as adopted children into your family."

Scripture

Ephesians 1: 4-8 (NAS)

Just as He chose us in Him before the foundation of the world, that we would be holy and blameless before Him. In love He predestined us for adoption as sons through Jesus Christ Himself according to the kind intention of His will to the praise of the glory of His grace, which He freely bestowed on us in the Beloved.

-

Question

Why go around with a piece of the problem stuck in your neck or buried under your skin when you have a Father who waits and wants to help you and give you freedom and life?

Chapter Five

Connections

The woods were full of sound as we made our way up from the Falls House towards the bridge. It seemed as though the whole earth was alive with sound busting out to announce the day. The only one silent in the woods appeared to be Luther. Half wolf and half husky, it was his nature to walk the woods in silence. The whoosh, whoosh of my snow shoes on the crusted snow, the chattering squirrels running on ahead in the tops of the trees and the blue jays announcing our arrival were just the chorus to the symphony the rest of nature sang to us that day. Our final destination was the car which was a mile and a half away.

Luther often ran ahead of me always staying where he could see me.   We had a connection and although I could not always see him I always knew he was there. If I needed him all I had to do was say his name. I did not even need to call out most of the time. He behaved much differently in the woods then he did in public. He ran free when we walked through the woods until we got to the bridge that crossed Dustin Brook.

The brook comes out of the beaver pond at the head of the trail and winds its way down through the woods across the back of the property behind the Falls House. The Falls House was my camp in the woods. It was octagon in shape and looked like a tar paper shack on the outside, but on the inside it was a light and airy space. It had a small storage loft over the kitchen and a sleeping loft over half the living space. The house had no electricity. The brook which cascaded over huge rocks fell about 60 feet just below the kitchen window provided the only running water. It was the most creative writing space I have ever been in.

When Luther arrived at the bridge he would stop and wait for me to catch up and fasten his lead onto his collar. That lead was his concession to going out into public. It made him feel safe and made me confident he could not step out of character and intimidate other animals or humans. He was not aggressive but he was intimidating because of his color and his stature. He looked like a wolf and I think he knew that.

White Birch, old hardwoods and evergreens make up our woods and the sun was playing tag with the shadows on the fresh snow. Suddenly there was only one sound. That whoosh sound of my snow shoes. All other noise had stopped as though the whole woods was taking a deep breath. I stopped and slowly looked around. What caused this interruption? Why the silence?

Luther stood as though at attention, perfectly still, stretching his nose and ears forward, lifting one paw then silently putting it down. He was turned looking past me into the woods. I turned slowly so as not to call attention to us, moving my body to face the direction he pointed.

He lowered his body slightly and slowly stepped forward one foot and then the other and stopped. As we stood watching, a doe and a half-grown fawn stepped into the clearing made by the path we were walking. She was nibbling on low hanging branches. Lunch for Luther! Awe and joy for me!

I could sense Luther's natural instincts taking over. Somehow, I knew in my heart he would not answer that call unless I released him to it. He was restrained by his own willingness to please me and to obey me. We were connected soul to soul.

Mother and child moved on across the clearing going deeper into the woods. Still Luther stood on point. "Breathe," I told myself. "Breathe." Luther's only restraint was our connection.

I turned towards Luther. "Come on boy, let's go." He looked at me as though he was a bit disappointed and then he sprinted up the trail ready for a tumble in the snow or a snow ball toss. What a joy he was to play with and to watch in the woods. Our connection was even stronger than I thought.

When I remember this story, it reminds me of our connections with each other and with God. I think about how as parents we want our children to do what we know is best for them and to follow the guidelines we have given them. Like Luther's freedom in the woods and his leash in public, God our Father doesn't want to restrain us His children, but teach us to choose what is best for ourselves and for others.

Throughout the New Testament we find Jesus going off by Himself to connect with His Father. Like Jesus we too need to find and keep the connection open with God the Father.

Prayer

"Jesus, I thank you for being my connection and for always being there to connect us with the Father. Thank you for giving your life so we can become totally connected."

Scripture

(Mark 1:35 NAS)

"Early in the morning while it was still dark Jesus got up and left the house and went to a secluded place and was praying there ."

Question

Who are you connecting with and how often are your lines open? Are you connecting with the heavenly Father?

Chapter Six

Bands of Steel

I was going to speak at church on Sunday so I thought I should wear my Sunday- Go-To-Meeting best. That meant I needed to put on one of my two skirts. Oh boy! Panty hose were in order for these white flaky legs. Now truth be known, I had not worn a skirt in at least three years. As for panty hose or tights, I only wear them to keep my legs warm under jeans or under slacks to dress up when I am speaking at events such as conferences and retreats.

Well, I still had some in the box brand new. You know the kind that are called "Legs." I usually keep a new box on hand just for the times I really need to dress up because when I wear them, they are always getting what my grandmother called "ladders". Those are the kind of "runs" that you just can't hide, the ones that usually end up with half your foot sticking out through the hole. Then you end up losing circulation due to the twisting tightness of the mesh around your foot.

When you are speaking you can't just take your pantyhose off, especially if you have them on under dress pants. You try to loosen them from around your foot which actually makes the hole bigger and allows it to slide up the back of your leg. Now you

have one leg hanging out from under your pants
and the other leg still intact.

You can always hope for some music so you can
dance around a bit and pull them up so that the toe
doesn't stick out from the bottom of your pant leg.
That is not likely to happen. You have to make
your story or speech so interesting and dramatic
that no one notices when you reach down inside
your pants to pull it up. Suddenly you realize that
is not a good idea. Now the hole is up on your thigh
and your leg is going numb. You finish your talk
and try not to drag your hind foot as you walk away
from the podium. You hope no one notices the toe
sticking out from the back of your pant leg.

The other scenario that happens to me is the one
where the panty hose really aren't the size that is
marked on the box. Instead of the "talls" they are
for very short people, those people with legs only a
foot or two long. They are made of spring steel.
You work at stretching them up over your knees.
You sit down and you pull them on one leg at a
time, stretching them as you go. Finally, you stand
up and hope that when you pull them up they will
go far. I mean clear up to your waist. It is
amazing, but they actually do. They are the ones
that make you look like you just lost 15 pounds and
you double check yourself in the mirror. Hey,
maybe you should wear these more often. You
finish getting ready. You put on a nice pair of dress
pants. The comfortable kind with the elastic in the

back where no one can see it under your jacket or sweater. It is important to have something on that is comfortable. You get in your car and drive to the location. You tug a little at your pants and jacket as you get out of the car. You smile and talk with people breathing more shallow than usual because of the tightness of the spring steel. You sit down hoping that the steel stretches a little to give you breathing room.

Then it is time for your talk. You walk up to the stage and you know that you are looking good. You begin to talk hoping your voice doesn't sound too high or strained. Suddenly everything loosens up a bit and you can breathe again. You gasp for air and smile. Nothing matters except the fact that you now can breathe and you can share your story.

What happened? Did that steel really stretch out a bit? It doesn't matter how it happened, you are just happy it did. You really get into your talk. It is only then that you realize those short legs are beginning to contract down! You reach behind you and pull up the slacks that are going down with the panty hose. You reach down and pull on the waist band of steel. It is like a spring. You pull it up and it pulls back down. It is a tug of war. A war you are not winning. You finish your story and as you walk off the stage you hold onto the waist band of your slacks. Smiling and laughing so no one will notice the way you are walking or the fact that by now the steel legs have contracted to their original height of two feet and the crotch has gone south with it.

That Sunday I thought of all those things. How I wanted to look my best to honor my audience and to honor God.   I got the Legs out of the box. I figured if these were the "steel" kind it wouldn't matter because I was going to wear a skirt and surely they wouldn't recoil down past my knees. My skirt was long. I sat down on the stool to put them on. They were black. My white flaky legs would not show under these that was for sure. I was going to look good. I stretched one toe out and put my left foot in. I pulled that leg up to my knee.

Suddenly a shadow fell. Well, Shadow didn't really fall. He jumped. He grabbed the end of one leg and began to pull. OH NO! It was another kind of tug of war. I had one foot in up to the knee. He had the other foot and was trying to run away with it! I started to yell "Hey cat, give that back!" Then I began to laugh. I pulled my leg out of the Legs and let go. Shadow took off. Those elastic bands of steel started to fly at him. He had one of his claws caught in the mesh and he struggled to get away. I was laughing too hard to be of much help.

I realized that the skirt I was planning to wear with those panty hose was probably going to go into someone else's closet soon and that what I really needed was to wear some cool sox with it.

It really isn't about dressing up to please me or because someone else thinks I should. It is about looking the best I can to honor the audience and to do honor to God. When I am asked to speak at church or other places, it is an honor and it is humbling. I want to give honor to God and those who care enough to listen.

I told a story about connections that morning and started with the story about Shadow and Legs. Shadow is 10 years old and he doesn't play much. He probably won't be playing with Legs again anytime soon.

I think it was a God thing. One of those "Be still and know that I am God" moments (Psalms 46:10 NAS). He does have a sense of humor and He did remind me that it isn't about me or how I look. It is about Him and putting Him first.

Prayer

"I thank you Father for always keeping the connections open between us."

Scripture

Psalm 25:4-5 (NAS)

Make me know your ways, O Lord: Teach me your paths, lead me in your truth and teach me for you are the God of my salvation. For you I wait all day.

Question

In what ways do you honor God? How do you show honor to those you care about?

Chapter Seven

The Guardian

I don't remember a time when I didn't do some kind of work. I started babysitting outside the home when I was eleven years old. I have had five successful careers and many odd jobs.

As a young mother I took care of twelve kids in my home. They call that a daycare now days. I have worked in restaurants across the country as well as nursing homes and hospitals. I have raised dogs and trained horses. I even set fence on a ranch in Oklahoma.

All the time I was learning new things, learning about faith, trust and love. Some of those lessons came through adversity, some came through miracles and others just came to me slowly over time.

Learning about trust was like that. It didn't happen all at once nor did I even recognize the lessons until years later.

One incident I distinctly recall happened while I was setting fence on a ranch in Oklahoma. My husband, Drew the ranch owner and myself were setting fence on Drew's ranch which covers thousands of acres. We were fencing in a quarter section of land which is about 460 acres.

37

When you "set fence" you dig holes, set posts in them, fill them with rocks and dirt and then string wire (usually barbed wire in those days) from one post to the next.   One of the reasons we were fencing in this quarter section was for the cattle that Drew was bringing down from the high range to pasture there in the fall. Another reason was the nearly wild horses that he kept on that range. He buys and sells cattle and sometimes he trades or sells horses. He uses horses extensively on the ranch. These horses were ones he left out in the pasture and he did not want them roaming too far off.

A few years before, Drew had turned loose a golden palomino stallion and a few rogue mares. The palomino stallion was a beautiful honey color with a blaze on his forehead and three white socks. Drew got him in a trade and soon discovered that this horse was stubborn and bull headed and would take a long time and a lot of training. There is an old saying, "One white sock, buy him; two white socks, try him; three white socks, shy away; and four white socks, give him away."

He learned that this stallion had been born out in pasture and had run free until the day before he was brought to the auction. Drew had a few options. He could sell him off; he could geld him; he could shoot him and cut his losses, or he could turn him out to pasture with some trusty mares and let him do the rest. That last option seemed the best and the least offensive. He was smart, strong and beautiful and should throw some beautiful colts. Drew planned to mark the foals each year and when they were three years old he would cull the herd, train some for use on the ranch and sell the others. This would keep the herd healthy.

He loaded the stallion into the trailer with a few of the breeder mares. They drove for about 45 minutes then pulled into a gate and closed it behind them. They pulled up to a three-sided pole barn. Drew and his ranch hand filled one end of the barn with hay and put some grain in the manger. He wanted the horses to come back to the barn for food occasionally. They opened the back of the trailer. The mares were nervous and Drew could see why. That stallion had somehow gotten his head out of his halter and was trying to turn around.

Drew backed the mares out first, one at a time, and led them to the grain in the barn. Then Drew and his ranch hand returned to the trailer to pull the pin and slide open the gate that held the stallion. They both got out of the way fast.

The stallion wasn't sure what to do at first. When he realized that the gate was gone he turned around ready for a fight. Drew talked quietly to him. The stallion moved slowly toward the open ramp to the trailer. He huffed with nervousness then jumped out clearing the ramp. He saw the mares and the grain. Drew said he looked torn between the mares, the grain and the open spaces of the huge pasture. The open land won that day. As they watched he ran off and then came back. He stood at a distance and watched as Drew and his ranch hand closed up the trailer, got in the truck and drove out the gate, locking it behind them.

That had happened seven years before we were there setting fence, repairing old fence and expanding the pasture.

The days were hot and dry and this day was no exception. The sun was straight up which meant lunch time. I got out the sack lunches and put them on the tail gate of the pickup. I poured myself a cup of coffee from the thermos. I started walking towards the rock that had been calling my name. I love to sit on rocks. I always have.

Drew and my husband were talking about the two three-year-old horses we were going to take as part of our pay. As I walked away, Drew called, "Be careful Lauretta." I thought he was talking about rattle snakes that are prevalent in that part of the country and I raised my stick. He laughed. "That stick won't do much good against that stallion!" He pointed behind me.

Standing off on a little rise was the most beautiful golden creature I had ever seen. The sun glistened off his coat. He seemed to be watching us for a minute then turned and was gone.

"I wondered when he would show up," Drew called. "He always comes to investigate whenever work is being done or hay brought in. He is the guardian and defender of his herd."

I went to my rock and sat down with my back to the sun. I opened my sack and took out the peanut butter and jelly sandwich that was my favorite lunch for hot days. I took a sip of my coffee, set the cup on the rock beside me and looked out over the land we had been working. "How beautiful the earth is," I thought. Even the dry red clay that stuck to our clothes and hands was beautiful to me.

I must have been sitting with that "300 mile" stare longer than I thought because suddenly I felt as though I was being watched. My senses became heightened. I heard cautious footsteps. My right hand reached slowly over and clutched the snake stick that I kept ever by my side. The footsteps stopped. I waited and they started up again slowly. My spirit calmed. I breathed as normally as I could. I could hear the huff of air from nostrils. I looked up and saw Drew reaching for his rifle. My husband said something to him and he stopped with the gun half raised.

Still I waited slowing my breaths, trying to quiet my heart. The stallion was right behind me. He reached out and took ahold of my shoulder with his teeth. Pulling at my shirt he pinched the skin underneath. I wanted to jump and run but something inside me was telling me to wait. Finally he let go. He whiffed again then slowly he stretched out his great neck and rested that beautiful head on my shoulder. I sat quiet and still.

I spoke softly to him and finally I slowly reached up and touched that scarred old face. It was rough and soft at the same time. I will never forget that feeling. It has been imprinted in my palm. We held each other suspended in time for what seemed like an hour. Suddenly he jerked his head back, snorted and was gone as fast as he had appeared. It had all been so dream-like that if it wasn't for the sting of my shoulder I wouldn't have been sure it had actually happened.

I sat for a few minutes and finished my coffee. I picked up my cup and walked back to the truck. No one said anything at all. We went back to setting fence. It was all in a day's work.

On the ride back to the ranch house, Drew said that was the first time the palomino had gotten near anyone since he had been turned loose. He said the stallion didn't trust anyone, but that you would see him when you brought in feed or new animals. He had fathered some beautiful foals. He guarded his herd and his territory. He would try to steal the three-year olds back when they cut them out of the herd in the fall, especially if they were fillies. He was scarred from battle with predators and other stallions. He was the guide and the guardian of the herd.

We too need a guide and a guardian. God is our guide and our guardian. He will fight for us. Sometimes He will stand at a distance and we will know He is watching over us. The difference is that God can and will always be there for us. He is not afraid. He stands firm and we do not have to jump and run away. His love is unconditional and we can always trust Him. We can let Him guide us anywhere He wants us to go.

Prayer

"Father God, thank you for always being there for me and for teaching me to trust you. Thank you for sending your guardian angels to watch over me and your Holy Spirit to guide me."

Scripture

Jeremiah 29:11(NAS)

For I know what plans I have for you declares the Lord, plans for welfare and not calamity, plans to give you hope and a future.

Question

Who do you trust? Who is your guardian?

Chapter Eight

Nothing But Blood.

There has only been one or maybe two times that I can remember wanting to pass out at the sight of blood, and it wasn't my own blood that caused that feeling.

The one I always remember was when I was a young mother. You have heard a lot about my only child. It happened when my daughter was 5 years old and just starting kindergarten. We lived in a small town in Kansas at the time and we had some rough and tumble neighbor boys who were the same age and a bit older.

My girl loved to play outside. She wasn't exactly what you would call a tomboy though. She loved dresses and curls in her hair. She also knew that she could do anything any of the boys could do. I don't think she even thought in gender terms. She climbed the tree in the back yard. She crawled around on the ground with the boys and she was probably the best cowboy. She played trucks and loved to play with the train set her dad got for her and him for Christmas.

In Kansas there were places I had told her she was not to play. There were things in Kansas that could hurt kids. Things like diamond back rattle snakes and brown recluse spiders. I was not too worried about the snake population because we had a dog that watched for them and would bark and bounce around it if he saw one until one of us went out to see what the commotion was and took care of the problem.

Brown recluse spiders were a different story altogether. They did not warn of their presence like the rattler did. Brown Recluse spiders usually hang out in crumbling wood and dark places. Our neighbor got bit by one when he had his truck up on the lift and was fixing it. It must have been in the fender or frame. It dropped down his sleeve and bit him on the arm. His arm turned black where he was bitten and he had to have it treated for quite a while. He almost lost that arm.

There was an old trailer frame in the back yard between our houses and the kids liked to go under it and pretend it was their fort. I had told her she could not go there. Every once in a while she would be playing with the boys and forget. One day she crawled under there and lifted her head up and banged it on the steel of the frame.

She came running in the house yelling and crying. Her hand was all covered with blood. I thought it was her hand that was hurt. I took her into the bathroom and began to wash her hand off, but I could not see where the blood was coming from. Then I noticed that it was running down her neck onto her shirt. Her head was bleeding, not her

45

hand. Head wounds bleed profusely and that one was no exception. I got a cold wash cloth and began to see where the blood was coming from. I soon realized that this was one cut that was going to take some stitches.

We suffer sometimes because of the choices we make and sometimes because of the choices others make.

I had her hold the cloth to her head and took her the few blocks to the hospital where our doctor's office was. He happened to be in at that time and rushed her into a room. She had stopped crying and began asking what stitches were going to look like and could she get a pretty band aid like she did when she got a shot?

They shaved that spot on her head and gave her a local shot to numb the site. I started to feel sick to my stomach. She laid very still while the doctor put the stitches in. I had to look away and took a drink of water. She was sitting up and I was finding myself sitting down with the nurse holding my head between my knees to keep me from passing out. I had been working in health care since I was a candy striper at the age of sixteen. I had assisted in surgery, worked in ER and seen all kinds of things and almost fainting made me feel down right stupid.

I guess it is harder to see one of your own suffering from injury or pain. I know I had a hard time when she was in labor giving birth to her first son. She was there so long and her pain got harder and harder. It was tough to watch. When it was over and we got to hold that child, I just wanted to sing. The baby was precious and knowing that my daughter was going to be okay made my whole being want to celebrate.

I bet that is how our Father feels when He sees His children suffer. I know God wants what is best for us and does not want us to suffer. I bet the angels cried with God when they saw His Son suffer and die. I know they sang when the stone was rolled away and He walked among the living again, and I can just imagine the celebration when He returned to them to sit next to God His Father.

Seeing God in the pain is difficult because He does not cause pain. Seeing God through the pain is wonder filled because He loves us so much. Like when Lesa came running in the house to me when she cut her head, we also go running to God when we hurt. Why? Because He loves us. He will give us comfort and heal us and He will not faint.

Prayer

"Father, thank you for giving us free choice. Help me to use it well."

Scripture

Romans 8:15 (NAS

For you have not received a spirit of slavery leading to fear but you have received a spirit of adoption as sons by which we cry "Aba, Father".

Questions

What kinds of choices have you made lately? How often do you run to the Father when you hurt? Do you run to Him with your Joy as well?

Chapter Nine

One Stop Shopping

It has been said that I am an unusual woman. I guess there are many reasons for that but the main one I can think of is that I hate to shop. Well hate is a rather strong word. Let's just say that I don't like it one bit and will wait until I can do it with a friend to make it fun or until I absolutely have to get something from the store before I go.

I don't like to window shop unless it is Christmas and the windows are decorated and fun to look at. If you find me going to the mall it means I have a very good reason. I have only been in the mall in our town two or three times in twenty years. That was because the thing I needed was only to be gotten there. Funny thing about that is, one of my successful careers was as a retail manager. I am much better at serving others than waiting for someone to serve me.

On the other hand I like to go into small craft shops and see what everyone is making to sell. I should be banned from book stores and quilt shops because I can easily waste a day in each one.

As for those big one stop shopping stores? Whoever invented them did not have me in mind when they did it. I dread going there especially when it is busy. People grab things from your hand and push and shove. You know at first glance that

49

the cashier doesn't like you and that you must have forgotten half of what you came in for. The conversation goes like this

You: "Hello"

Clerk: "Did you find everything?"

You: "You can't lie to her so you say "No, but that is okay."

Clerk: "What did you forget?"

You: "I didn't forget anything."

Clerk: "You just said you didn't find everything!"

You: "I didn't find everything but that is okay, I guess I don't really need it.""

Clerk: "Well what was it you forgot?"

You: "I didn't forget… oh never mind dried prunes."

Clerk: (shouts) "Hey Jesse go get this lady a package of dried prunes."

You: "No, that is okay" (now the whole world knows you need prunes)

Clerk: (shouts to the line forming behind you) "It will be a couple of minutes folks, this lady forgot her prunes."

You can't decide whether to jump over the counter and club her with the jug of milk, or to crawl into the bottom of the carriage and push your cart outside. You do neither. You wait for the guy who went to get you some dried prunes while the people behind you whisper and stare holes in your back. He can't find the dried prunes either and asks loudly if you really need them.

You stop the clerk from calling anyone else and pay for what you have found and go load the stuff in your car.

One of the women who was in line behind you stops by your car to commiserate with you about the need for dried prunes and makes other suggestions! She says "My mom always swore by prunes. Said they kept her regular."

You smile and thank her and get in your car. You look in the mirror. Do you look like you need prunes? Suddenly it all seems too funny. You begin to giggle and then to laugh out loud.

There is actually only one real "One Stop Shopping" experience that I love and that is with my heavenly Father. His word really does have all the answers we seek. He is my One Stop Shopping. I can take every request to Him. He can fill the prescriptions, help with my stress, take care of my family, bless my grandkids, and teach me to love.

Prayer

"Father thank you for supplying all my needs."

Scripture

Psalms 34: 8-10 (NAS)

O taste and see that the Lord is good: How blessed is the man who takes refuge in him. O Fear the Lord you his saints for those who fear him there is not want. The young lions do lace and suffer hunger but those who seek the Lord shall not be in want of any good thing.

Question

What is your One Stop Shopping like?

Chapter Ten

It Happens Like That.

They say, "Life happens when you are making other plans." I say you make plans and God laughs. He knows the plans He has for you. He has promised wonderful things and He always keeps His promise. Sometimes the way you get there is the long way around though.

Here I am making plans for the day. I know God is laughing. My plans change as often as I change my mind. I wouldn't exactly say I was indecisive. I would say a woman has a right to change her mind. Probably 20 times a day is stretching it though. Hey! I am not the only one. Well maybe 20 times a day is an exaggeration.

I do have a tendency to bounce from one thing to another and one project to the other. To counteract my over activity and my lack of what others sometimes call focus, I make lists.

Some days those lists are very detailed. Sometimes they are so generic I have to focus to know what I meant to do, but in the end they usually get mostly done.

There are always some things that can be put off to tomorrow until they finally get to the top of the list. Like your laundry for instance. Sometimes you just need certain clean things. I know a guy who buys new socks and underwear when his old ones are all dirty. Occasionally he does a whole washer full of socks and underwear just so he can say he did the laundry.

Now there is a secret to making lists. You can do it two ways. One is to categorize your lists and get very detailed. That way it looks like you have a lot to do and you do. It also gives you a chance to check more things off so you get that sense of accomplishment that you did a good job.

The second way is to just write down random stuff and do them as you see fit. I like that one best. I can prioritize.

My today's list went like this:

Get up DONE
Make the bed DONE (one of my friends says why make it, you just mess it up when you get in it again anyway)
Eat breakfast DONE
Read and meditate on God's word. DONE BEFORE BREAKFAST
Write in my journal. DONE DURING BREAKFAST
Write the book. WORKED AN HOUR
Study reference material for the Sarah's Quilts story. DID SOME
Make soup for lunch. DONE
Write the book. WORKED AN HOUR AND A HALF
Eat the soup. DONE

Write the book. NOT DONE. PICKED UP JO'S KIDS FROM SCHOOL

Practice a story for Monday. DONE KIDS LOVED THE STORIES.

Clean the living room.

Write the book.

Dance. DONE. KIDS LIKE TO DANCE TOO!

Write the book.

Exercise. HEY, AT LEAST I DANCED

Go out to dinner with friends - YUMMY

Read over list and move undone items to top of next day. OH BOY!

As you can see the plans I had made all changed. I needed to help a friend. I tried to practice the story for Monday in the car on the way. I think its okay to stop what I am doing and be gone for an hour or two to help a friend. Besides, when a friend calls or even a neighbor who hasn't really been very neighborly needs something aren't you supposed to help if you can? Don't I ask God each morning to show me where I can be a blessing to someone?

I do have a tendency toward procrastination, especially where getting this book done is concerned. This isn't procrastination though. My friend really did need help. She had to take one of her kids to the doctor and she needed me to pick up the others from school and take them home. It didn't take long. Besides I did practice my stories on the kids. They love stories too. Oh and boy do they love to dance. Maybe this is where the scripture in Matthew that says "Do unto others as you would have them do unto you" comes in.

Prayer
"Thank you God for showing me ways TO DO things that help others."

Scripture

Luke 6:31 (NAS)

Do unto others as you would have them do unto you.

This scripture holds the truth of a happy God filled life. If we treat others the way we want to be treated we will be working in God's will and be blessed by His grace.

Question
How is your TO DO LIST coming?

Chapter Eleven

God Has a Sense of Humor

God has a sense of humor. I know because I see so many funny things in nature and in my life. So many funny God things. He has to be smiling or laughing a lot of the time.

There are so many funny stories in my life it is hard to pick which ones to tell you. I guess I will start with one a friend we will call Mary told me recently. She says it is positively true and I can see it happening many times over. Here is what she told me.

A friend of Mary's was at work when she received a phone call from the school asking her to come pick up one of her children who had quite a high fever. Then she called Mary and asked if she would pick up her other two children when she picked up her own kids from school and watch them while she dealt with her sick child.

Mary said, "I did just that. I didn't mind. We both watch each other's children on occasion and whatever her son had, my kids were already exposed to."

First Mary's friend took her son to the doctor and then took him home and tucked him in. He was not a happy boy. He had a sore throat and a shot just made the other end hurt too. Her husband came home from work and she left to go to the pharmacy. She was stopping at the grocery store for soup and ice cream before she came to pick up her other children.

When she came out of the grocery store she found that in her haste she had locked her keys in the car. She looked around. There were not many people in the store and no one in the parking lot. She found an old coat hanger over by the bushes. Someone else had done this too! She tried to shove the coat hanger in the door but just couldn't do it.

She bowed her head and said "God, I don't know how to do this. Please send me some help."

She was just about to go into the store and ask the manager for help when a motorcycle pulled up beside her. The rider was a bearded man with a cap on his head and he was sporting a black leather jacket with a skull and cross bones on the back. He asked if she needed help.

"Well, yes I do!" she said and went on to explain about the sick child and the ice cream and that she locked her keys in the car. He listened patiently and finally she said "I found this, do you know how to use it to open my car?"

"Sure thing." he said and walked around to the side of the car. Within a minute it was unlocked and he handed her the keys and the coat hanger.

She hugged him. "Thank you so much, you are a godsend and a very nice man."

He says "Lady, you got that wrong, I am not a nice man. I just got out of prison yesterday. I was in prison for car theft."

She hugged him again and said "Thank you God, I asked for help and you sent me a professional!" Mary said her friend was still smiling at the look on his face when she got to her house to pick up the other kids.

I laughed when my friend told me this story and I promised not to pass the names on. I have heard other stories like this before. Some involved tires that went flat or cars that had slid into the ditch. In all of them the most unlikely person becomes the hero.

On another note this was not the first time Mary's friend has locked her keys in the car. Nor is it the first time I did such a thing. I locked my stuff in the car one cold winter night when I was performing

and had to call my roadside service to come unlock
it. They were busy because it was a dark and
stormy night. Thank goodness they got there before
I was to perform and I could get my sound system
out and set up in time. Of course, that put me on
edge. I think I had to tell the audience about it just
so they could laugh and get me moving toward the
stories I was there to tell.

Another time, I took my little sister out to lunch
and to the fabric store. They were side by each in
the strip mall and we had to decide which one to go
into first. The food won that time as we were both
hungry. When we were finished, we had a short
disagreement about who was to pay the bill but we
both laughed when I won and went to pay the bill
only to discover not only had I left my keys in the
car, but my purse as well. She said it was a trick to
get her to pay. Of course she was teasing. The car
had locked itself after I shut the door, probably
because I had left the keys in the ignition. She had
roadside service that time. So I waited until they
came and unlocked the car before I joined her in the
fabric store. She has not let me forget that one.
Just when I think she has forgotten, she quips,
"Have you got your keys?" as we get out of the car.

I have locked myself out of the car so many times
that my fella has hidden a key where I can find it
and gotten me an extra one to carry in my purse.
Trouble with the extra key is remembering to move

it when I change bags. Funny, since he got that done for me, I have not locked myself out! Must be a security thing, just knowing that I have that extra key somewhere. It is sort of like having a security blanket. Now if I can just remember where he put that extra key.

Just knowing I have a key makes me feel secure. Just knowing I have a God who cares makes me know I am secure. It isn't a simple feeling. It is a knowing deep down in my spirit that touches the very core of my existence. A knowing that I have a Father who loves me! Just as I am! Knowing if I fall He will pick me up. That I will never be locked out of His presence.

Prayer

"God, thank you for making me feel secure in you and your love."

Scripture

Matthew 11:28-30 (NAS)

Come to me all you who are weary and burdened, and I will give you rest. Take my yoke upon you and learn from me, for I am gentle and humble in heart, and you will find rest for your souls. For my yoke is easy and my burden is light.

Question

Who is your security blanket? Where do you find your rest?

Chapter Twelve

Focused

 I have always been one who has a whole lot of things going on at the same time. My mother and my grandmother used to say things like "take it one thing at a time Lauretta," or "Focus on your homework" or "Stop daydreaming and focus on what you are doing."

I have always had a problem with doing just one thing at a time. As a young mother I thought learning to focus would be a good thing to try to do. I read the books and even took a class at one time on focusing. In the late 60's we moved to Kansas to be close to my younger sister and her family. It was soon apparent that I needed something like a job to focus on while my daughter was in school.

I started out as a waitress at Mary & Wanda's Cafe in Wellington, Kansas. When I started, they were in a small building not far from where we lived. I could walk to the cafe and work during the hours my daughter was in school, so it was a good fit.

The building was way too small for the amount of business they had at lunch time. There was always a line out the door of people waiting for a seat or standing in line for takeout orders. We did them on a first come, first served basis and often people ordered the same things every day.

There was a lunch counter with eight stools and a small room to the side that held five tables. One of them was round and that was where Mary and Wanda took their breaks and planned the week's menu. There was always fried chicken, french fries, hamburgers and salad on the menu. Every week they would also include a different special that was not on the written menu. I was only there a week when I suggested that we use some of the take-out boxes to put salads up ahead so people could also buy them to take back to work. They went like hot cakes and we began putting Mary's secret dressing in little plastic containers to go with the salad. This speeded the line up so people didn't have to take time at the counter to put dressing on their salad. It was important to get food to our customers as quickly as possible so they could get back to work on time.

Mary's dressing was famous. People came from as far away as Tulsa, Oklahoma to buy it by the pint. Business people had offered to buy the recipe and she had refused. She had purchased it from her uncle when they had bought the business from him and promised to keep it a secret. Mary was a woman who kept her word. She did not even let Wanda know what was in the secret ingredients she added to the mayo and french dressing combination that she used as a base. She would go in the kitchen and send everyone out. She would take something from here, another thing from there and mix a few ingredients together. The result was phenomenal. Love was the secret ingredient I think. Mary really loved her work and the people she served.

It had taken a few years to grow their business, but the two women had stayed focused on their plans and now it had outgrown the space. I moved out of town to the horse ranch, but continued to work a few days a week. They moved to the other end of town to the old train station. They kept the business going in the old place through all the renovations right up to the week they moved. They feared they might lose the lunch crowd, but the regular customers came with them and they soon had a dinner crowd as well.

The train came by four times a day as regular as clock work and it added to the ambiance of the place. People would bring their kids in for lunch so they could see the trains go by. It made the day for many a little boy and girl.

I don't really remember too much about the decor except that there was a lot of orange. There was a long counter with 12 stools in front of the kitchen pass through and a large open dining area that held about 20 tables. They hired another waitress and I learned to cook.

It was soon acknowledged that I would not make a good breakfast cook, but I could do lunch and dinner like a pro. I just could not get the eggs right no matter what I did. Wanda tried a few times to show me how. She kept saying "Focus on the yolk." No matter how hard I tried to focus on that little orange ball, something else would distract me and I would break it or get it over done or take it off too soon. About the only eggs I got perfected were omelets and scrambled. Soon I was doing prep and cooking for lunch and dinner and waiting tables as needed.

I was also focused on the ranch. It wasn't long after we moved that I had also been given that responsibility because my husband worked on the railroad and was gone most of the time. He would be home two or three weekends a month and then he had friends who came to ride horses. Soon I was boarding horses and working only a day or two a week at the restaurant. I loved the people who came in to the restaurant on a regular basis and they would be sure to come when I was working just to say hi.

We had one man who always ordered the chili with bread, the salad with crackers and a plate of fried chicken for lunch. He was a tall skinny guy and I wondered where he put all that food. He never wasted any of it.

There was a woman who was deaf and wore hearing aids that came for breakfast every day. She lived alone and walked everywhere she went. You would see her all over town. She always carried a bright colored purse that had big flowers on it. Wanda asked her about it once and she said it didn't matter to her if it was in style or not or if it was summer or winter. She liked that purse and had repaired it twice. It made her smile with its big bright flowers and she needed a smile every now and then.

She always seemed to know exactly what she wanted and seemed to be focused on whatever her mission was each day. I don't know if she worked anywhere or not. I admired her cool, focused, put together attitude and thought she probably never had a care in the world.

I enjoyed being on the ranch and life was good for a while. It wasn't more than a year before things went downhill rapidly. I was having a tough time of it and wished I could be as focused and put together as that woman with the flowered purse. I was so wrong.

I remember this particular day was a Wednesday because I didn't usually work Wednesdays. Mary had asked me to come fill in for Wanda because she had to go to Wichita to pick up some things they needed at the cafe. I was working doing salad prep and waiting on the customers at the counter when the woman with the flowered purse came in later than usual.

I asked her if she wanted her usual and she said "No!" She ordered a big lunch. She had a bowl of chili and then a whole fried chicken dinner. I had to give her mashed potatoes because the baked potatoes weren't done yet. Funny the details you remember when something happens, isn't it?

I served her and talked with her for a couple of minutes. She smiled more than I had ever seen her smile. She finished eating. Got up and paid the bill. She left me a very generous tip. That was unusual and I asked her if she had made a mistake. Silly me, as a waitress you should never ask about a tip being too much.

She said "No, that was not a mistake. Use it to take care of that precious daughter of yours."

"Thank You." I said.

It was the last thing I said to her as she walked out the door. Her timing was impeccable. She walked out, stopped at the train tracks as the approaching train blew it's whistle. I watched as she reached up to her ears and did something to her hearing aids and then stepped out in front of the train. I shouted "NO!" But of course she did not hear me. The people in the restaurant jumped at my shout and came to the windows and door.

My eyes still fill with tears as I write this almost 50 years later. I never quite understood how she could do that. The woman who I saw as so focused and so put together really wasn't at all.

The engineer and conductor on the train said they saw her standing as though she was just waiting for the train. She had looked directly at the train before she stepped in front of it.

I think of her every once in a while. I still don't understand it. The Bible says in Deuteronomy 30:19 "This day I call the heavens and earth to witness against you that I have set before you life and death, blessings and the curse. So choose life in order that you may live, you and your descendants." (NAS)

I know that means choose Christ and life over evil and death, but in this instance all I could think of was that she made a choice for death. Here was a woman who seemed focused on life, but something had distracted her to the point that she chose death.

Years later when my daughter had grown and had a family of her own, I too came to a point where I had to make a choice. I was in the lowest place I had ever been emotionally and it looked like an easy fix to all the problems and loneliness I was facing. I didn't think of the woman at the train until afterward, but I think I understand it a bit more now. I could not just step out in front of the train literally or figuratively. I had God in my life even if I wasn't walking close to Him at the time. I did want to live, to work and to play another day. God doesn't make our decisions for us. He gives us the choice. He says, "I set before you life and death. Choose life."

Prayer
Father, I thank you for your saving grace and your love. I thank you for the knowledge and peace that gave me the courage to face another day and an uncertain future. Thank you for the ability to choose life and the help to overcome adversity. My life has been blessed beyond measure and my heart is full of the love you so readily give us.

Scripture
Psalms 59:9 (NAS)

Because of His strength I will watch for You, for God is my stronghold.

Questions
Have you ever questioned why you are here and why you are going through the things you are dealing with? Are you an overcomer?

Chapter Thirteen

Angels Unaware

Years ago, when my daughter was six years old, we lived on a farm in Kansas. I boarded and trained horses and my husband worked for the Atchison, Topeka and Santa Fe Railroad. He was a one of the laborers who went with a crew to fix the tracks wherever they were broken or needed new ties. He was gone a lot of the time while I was home taking care of the horses and our daughter.

It was a lot of work but I loved the farm and the horses. It kept me busy, that is for sure. I taught my daughter to ride and she was a natural. I exercised the horses, groomed them, fed them and fixed the fence when it was breached.

My husband wasn't sure he liked my being out there alone so much of the time. I had guns and I knew how to shoot them. Besides the only "snakes" we had out there were diamond back rattlers. I stepped on one barefoot in the middle of the night once. That snake was as terrified as I was. I never went barefoot out there again.

My husband used to come home on weekends and friends would come over and we would all ride. It was a good place to be most of the time. One

Saturday when we were hosting a large group of riders, the subject came up among the men about me being the one that trained a certain horse and about me being by myself most of the time. The majority was sure their wives could not do that. Especially the part of being alone and doing all the chores. It was sort of a bragging right for my husband I guess, but after they left, he got to thinking about it and it made him more uneasy.

I was not ready to leave this beautiful place that finally felt like home so we "discussed" it. I held my ground for once. We had already moved many times in our eight years of marriage and this was the first time I really felt at home.

The next weekend that he came home, he brought a man with him. He had picked him up hitchhiking. I liked the old guy right away so I didn't even question it. He often picked people up and brought them home for dinner and a sleepover before they went on their way. Life was more casual and transient in the sixties. I was trusting and naïve. The man said his name was Jake. He didn't offer a last name and we didn't ask. My husband told Jake that we needed a farmhand and if he wanted to stay for a while, we would give him room and board and pay him some as well.

Jake was a drifter. He said he preferred to be on the road but he would settle for a little while. If he liked it he would stay until the weather turned.   He looked old to me. I was in my early twenties so anything over fifty probably looked old. I never really found out how old he was. In fact, I didn't find out much about Jake.

He had at least one grown child. I knew that because he told stories about how my daughter reminded him of her and how once a year or so he would drop over to her house to visit and play with the grandkids. Seemed she always made the mistake of trying to make him settle down and stay with her.

I could see why. He was quiet and polite. He had tons of skills that were useful on a farm. I did not have to tell him what needed to be done. He would be up and out with the horses checking to see they had food and making sure everything was okay before my daughter was fed and ready for the day. He found things to do until I called him in for lunch.

Jake didn't eat breakfast. Said it would spoil him and he would become fat and lazy. I couldn't see how that would ever happen. He was lean and wirey. His face was the one you see in the old cowboy pictures with deep lines and a tan where his hat wasn't. The only time he took that hat off was at meal time. He said it wasn't polite to wear a hat at the table. He had a full head of snow white hair. He said he earned it. I think he wore that hat to bed. I never had the nerve to sneak in and check when he was snoring.

Besides all his other talents, Jake could play a mean bluesy ragtime piano. After supper every night he would take his coffee over to the piano and play. I was surprised the first time he did that. He had two fingers missing on his right hand. When I asked him about it, he said he just got his hand in a place it shouldn't be and got them shot off. He would not elaborate on that story at all.

I remember a lot of the songs he played. The tunes like Saint Louis Blues and House of the Rising Sun. He played old tunes from the 30's and 40's too. I absolutely loved it when he played boogey woogey blues. I could sit and listen to him for hours. The neighbor woman and her kids came to ride horses with us often and they heard him play one night and invited him down to their house on Saturday to join in with the family jam session. It's funny how musicians seem to find each other the same way storytellers do.

Jake stayed for a while. I got used to him being there. He built a new gate for the small pasture. He fixed the roof on the shed. He checked the fence periodically.
He helped me seine the small pond and he put the fish in the big pond for me. He helped me get the

hay in. I had to drive the truck though because he said he didn't have a driver's license. I didn't care. I liked driving the truck.

He patched the big cement horse tank and filled it with water so my daughter could have a swimming place. She loved it. It was a great place for her to cool off.

I missed him when he moved on. One day a cold wind came in from the north and it was fall already. He took his knapsack and I drove him into town. My husband wasn't home and I didn't have much money but I gave him what I had. I knew we owed him a lot more. Besides all the work he had done, he had been there when I really needed someone. He gave me a post office address for general delivery and told me to send him his pay when my husband got back.

He said he didn't do goodbyes so he would just say farewell. I dropped him off at the highway. I don't think he saw my tears as I drove away and he stuck out his thumb.

Jake called me one time and asked me to send him some money. Said he would give it back when he came back through. He was in Virginia and had been picked up for vagrancy. I didn't have much money either. I sent him what I could. I don't know if he ever came back through because my husband moved us again, first into town and then to another state. I imagine he did though. He seemed to be the kind of man who would keep his word.

My guardian angel's name was Jake that summer. I think it was a "God thing". Because he was there, my husband didn't move us into town until later. I got the whole summer to just be who I wanted to be and where I wanted to be. I got to do the things I loved and I never worried about any harm coming to my daughter and myself.

Prayers
"Thank you God for angels unaware, especially one named Jake."

Scripture
Hebrews 1:14 (NAS)

Angels "are they not all ministering spirits, sent out to render service for the sake of those who will inherit salvation"

Questions

Are you aware of your guardian angels?

Chapter Fourteen

Choices

"It isn't the dark that is scary. In fact the scary part is having too much light." That is what she said when I asked her if she wasn't scared. I was shaking, I was so scared. This was my first dive.

"It is okay, no one cares if we come here. In fact, I think they sometimes add things that are better for us when they can."

I wasn't so sure about that. Dumpster diving was something I had not done before and I almost felt like I was doing something illegal or wrong. They said it wasn't stealing. It would all just go to the dump tomorrow anyway. I had seen the stuff go out the back door and knew a lot of it was good, untouched food.

I was hungry, but worse was the fact that I couldn't feed my daughter all the nutritional things that she needed. I got lunch from the restaurant I worked at but I saved it and took it home so she could have dinner. Usually it was fried chicken or chili, sometimes even a leftover baked potato. The days that I didn't work were hard. I had rent and utilities to pay and it took all that I made and sometimes there wasn't enough. I had 78 cents for gas to get to work that week. It was a good thing there was a gas war on then.

I took some spotted apples and a loaf of bread that was in a torn plastic bag. I also took some greens, an onion and a spotted tomato. Then I found a cuke and some cheese. I could cut the mold off the cheese and it was good protein. We would have salad for dinner tonight and my daughter's favorite, grilled cheese. There was some meat with a torn wrapper that I left. I knew that there were others who came here and besides, I wasn't as hungry as they were.

Jan was filling her sack. She had a lot of mouths to feed. Well let's just say, she found ways to feed a bunch of homeless people. I wasn't homeless at least. I helped her pick out whatever we could find that was good and not chewed on. She talked quietly while we worked. "This is going to make good soup and this apple sauce is going to Mrs. X for her baby." By the time we were done, I almost felt good about what we were doing.

Being hungry wasn't new to me. I remember as a child when we had eaten beans every way mom could fix them and were down to our last meal. She had not eaten for a couple of days to make sure her hungry kids had enough. Dad's meager pay from the church he pastored did not pay the bills let alone have much left over for food.

A friend of the family came for a visit and found mom crying in the kitchen. He was angry. He said the people at the church where my dad preached should have seen that we at least had food. He stormed off and later we found out he went to the elders of the congregation and made them raid their own food pantries. He came back with a truckload of food. Mom was overwhelmed.

Now here I was, dumpster diving to feed my daughter. Well, that was not going to happen too many times. I had made up my mind. I was not going to go through this for very long. I didn't mind helping Jan find food for the people she was helping. I sure wasn't going to live this way for long.

We finished behind the grocery store and went to the big green dumpster behind the fancy restaurant. There Jan found steak and potatoes and lots of salad fixings. No wonder she could feed so many. People just threw away a lot of good stuff. Here she said we had to be real quiet or we would have some trouble. Some of the bums that she didn't help claimed this spot as their own and would fight for it. She said it was good food, but it was not worth getting beaten up for.

I went home and gladly fixed supper with what I had gotten. I had a new resolve. I was not going to let this little bump in the road get me down. I was also not going to do this very long.

That night I really talked to God. I wanted to know how He could have let me get so destitute when He was always supposed to provide for our needs. I wanted to know where my husband was and why he had left us without the bills being paid and not come back when he said he would. He said he was out on a job but when I called, his boss told me he didn't work there any longer and hadn't for weeks. I wanted to know just what God was going to do about it.

Then I started making plans. I didn't wait for God to do anything. Looking back, I wish I had. It would have saved me years of struggle thinking I just wasn't doing enough. Having a low opinion of myself didn't help either. If I had only let go and let God take care of it all.

When I look back on those days so long ago and I see so many homeless people today I wonder, what has changed? Well for one thing we recognize the fact that there are destitute people in this county. We don't hide it or try to pretend it doesn't exist. There are a many shelters and food banks around the country, too. Not everyone goes to them and with the drug addiction crisis in this country, sometimes we can't do much. But we can give it to God.

It took me a long time to realize giving it to God did not mean talk to Him and ask for help and then take it back and do whatever I could think of. I know I would have struggled a lot less if I had stopped and waited for Him to help. He can't help if we don't let Him.

I also know that God does want us to do what we can. He will show us the way though. He wants us to let Him lead. That does not mean sit down and do nothing. It means ask for guidance and listen for that still small voice that gives us direction.

Sometimes while we are waiting to hear from Him, God handles the problems in other ways. Sometimes someone will come up to you and in talking give you the answer you have been waiting for. Other times it seems there is no answer and it looks as though God hasn't been listening. He has though and His timing is just not what ours is. When we wait upon Him, He will provide for us in ways we never dreamed.

Prayer
"Thank you God for showing me how to let go and let you do it. Thank you for showing me

what I can do and teaching me to let you do the
rest."

Scripture
Philippians 4:6 (NAS)

Be anxious for nothing, but in everything by
prayer and supplication with thanksgiving let
your requests be made known to God. My God
will supply all your needs according to His
riches in glory in Christ Jesus.

Question
What are you holding on to?

Chapter Fifteen

It Takes A Church

It just struck me the other day that what Paul says about us being the body of Christ in 1 Corinthians 12: 12 –31 is pretty important.

Christ was here in human form. He understood the workings of the body and so the analogy works. He went away and sent back the Holy Spirit so that we could remain in constant contact with Him.

Why would He do that? Because you always want to be in contact with those you love and He loves us enough to give up His life for us.

All of the parts of a body are important. There are very few that are disposable. The disposable ones are only that way because they collect the bad stuff that comes in and stores it so it can't contaminate the other parts of the body. Once those parts are full they can be discarded with the understanding that we make our bodies more vulnerable when they are. Those parts are things like your tonsils and your appendix.

Each part has its specific job. Your feet help you to balance and walk upright. Each part of your feet have their own job. Take your toes for instance. Your big toe is a balancing machine. Without it you would tip forward more. Your other toes are grippers. They help you grip onto things as you walk. The ball of your foot and your heel are parts of your support group. They help you stay upright and not reverse back to crawling. Your feet are very strong. They hold your whole body weight. They move you forward or backward. They can be used as tools to push or kick or stomp.

What about your legs? They can propel you forward and backward. They respond to the adrenalin that asks the question flight or fight in a startling situation. Sometimes it seems they have a will of their own. When you want to go to sleep, they want to cramp up. When you want to sit and relax they suddenly are up and going from one place to the other and getting you into something you did not think you were ready to do. They help to keep you upright. They help you see over other people's heads! Well maybe not if your legs are short. Yep, they come in all sizes too. Everything from tooth picks to beams.

Our inner workings are amazing and so are our arms, hands and brains

Each one has its own usefulness and each one does what God intended it to do. Perhaps we should take a lesson from our own bodies. Especially if we want to be part of the body of Christ.

Christ is the head of the church and therefore the head of the body. He is our leader, our savior and the brains of this organization called "Life in Christ".

The neck is the church as a whole. It holds up the head and connects the head to the body.

Each person in the congregation has a part in the body of the church. Just the same way that each member of the choir has its part to sing. Bass, tenor, alto and soprano all sing their own parts. When they sing together they become one whole sound. It would be very unusual for a bass singer to try to sing the soprano parts. It would mess the rest of the music up. That is the same way a body works.

It would look awful funny if a foot decided the head was getting more attention and wanted to be where the ear was, or the eye decided it was tired of looking around all the time and wanted to be down there on the knee. What if the ear would rather be the mouth?

When I was young I thought I wanted to go to Africa and become a missionary. A family of missionaries came to our camp and showed us pictures of Africa and all the people who needed God but didn't know Him. It was very romantic and I have always been a dreamer. I was sure that was the part I was going to play when I grew up.

I didn't know I was going to be a mother or live in many different places. I didn't know what part God had for me to play. Those parts have changed over the years just the same as we all change. "For everything there is a season a time for everything under heaven." Ecclesiastes 3:1 (NIV)

Each one in the body of Christ has their purpose at any given time. For some it is to be the head and for others it is to be the assistant to the head. For some it is to be an encourager and for another it is to be the dish washer or the sweeper. Each one is as important as the other. Without the encourager, the leaders could get a spirit of depression. Without the sweeper, the building would be a mess. There are as many places in the body of Christ as there are people in the church. Each one is different and brings different talents to serve. They key word is SERVE. We are to serve the body and because we all are part of the body, we are to serve each other.

Prayer

"Lord give us the courage and the knowledge to be whatever it is you want us to be. We know that you will not give us anything to do that you do not equip us for."

Scripture

I Corinthians 12:27 (NAS)

Now you are Christ's body, and individual members of it.

Question

What part do you play in the body of Christ?

Chapter Sixteen

Three Guys

I often tell stories in assisted living homes or nursing homes. I go to them because I love the people.

At one point I was booked to tell once a month at the same location. It was an assisted living place that housed people with dementia and Alzheimer's diseases, including those who just could not be alone anymore all the way to those at the end of life.

There were between 15 and 20 people who liked to come to listen to the stories. Among them were three men all with the same first name. We will call them all Henry. Although they have passed on, I do not know their families and would not be able to get permission to use their real names.

Henry 1 would meet me at the door each month. He was always dressed up with his cap and vest and tie. He dressed for all occasions. He would help carry my sound system into the room and take me by the arm to lead me in. I always stopped and waited for him. He loved to help. He was gracious and kind. He loved to listen to the stories and often got caught up in them.

Henry 2 would be waiting. First it was with his walker coming slowly into the area, getting ready to listen. He always had a smile and laughed at every story. He loved to laugh. He was genuine and happy. He sometimes laughed at the wrong places in a story or at stories that were not so funny but no matter the story, he would wait until the end and then he would really laugh. He especially liked one line jokes so I remembered to write some down to tell him.

Henry 3 played the harmonica. He also loved stories and often would tell me some of his own while I set up my sound equipment and got ready. Then he would say "Do you want me to play my harmonica for you?" I would reply "After I finish telling my stories you can play for me while I pack up okay?" He would smile and pat his pocket where he carried his harmonica.

He listened attentively and one time I told a story I had told a few months before. He said "I caught you!" I asked him what he had caught me at and he replied "You told that story about the snake before. I heard you!" I laughed and said something like sometimes people like to hear a story more than once. He said, "I like the story about the wolf and the mouse will you tell that one again next time?" Sure thing. I wrote it down in my notebook so I would not forget. I wondered how someone who was suffering from dementia could recall so clearly what I had done months before. I wouldn't remember what story I told from one month to the next unless I wrote them down.

While I packed up, Henry 3 would play his harmonica. At first, he would have trouble with the notes and the tune. After a few bars he would remember and get right into playing for me. When he played certain songs he would ask me to dance with him. He would get confused if I said yes because he could not play the harmonica and dance at the same time. I would smile and say "I have to go soon Henry so why don't you just play for me this time and we can dance later?" After I finished packing up, I would sit down and listen to a couple of his tunes. I would applaud and thank him for the music. Then he would point at me and say "Someday you and me is gonna dance." I would have danced with him any time he wanted if he could have figured out how to play and dance too but he wanted to dance to the music he made.

I think now that Henry 1 is greeting people as they come into heaven and Henry 2 is laughing and filled with joy and making angels shout with laughter at his jokes. As for Henry 3, I think he is playing in the band and sometimes he is dancing with the angels. Maybe one day I will get to see them all and dance with Henry 3.

I know that all three of these angels brought joy into my life. When my time at their facility was over, I missed them most. I saw God in all of them. I saw the graciousness and laughter and the music. The stories they loved to hear the best and the happiness an hour a month gave them brought me so much more than I brought to them.

There were a lot of other people at the facility and I have some stories from them too. Some of their stories I can tell and some I cannot because they asked me not to. Sometimes they would sit with me and talk for a while after I told my stories because something I said triggered a memory and they needed to tell it. They told them because they needed to. I was trusted and privileged to hear them. I listened because I wanted to and I knew that was what God would want me to do.

God puts people in our lives for a season. Sometimes they last a lifetime but more often they are here in our lives for a while and then gone on to other places and other things. We often do not know how we will bless others just by being there or how we will be blessed by the people that come into our life. I have been blessed many times over by people like the three Henrys. They taught me much and made me laugh. As I think of them today I am still smiling.

Prayer

"Father help me to see the stories in all of us and to tell the most important story of all at the perfect time. The story of your Son."

Scripture

Ecclesiastes 3: 1-8 (NAS)

To everything there is a season and every
blessing under heaven.
A time to be born and a time to die;
A time to plant and a time to uproot;
A time to kill and a time to heal;
A time to tear down and a time to build up;
A time to weep and a time to laugh;
A time to mourn and a time to dance;
A time to scatter stones and a time to gather
stones;
A time to embrace and a time to refrain;
A time to search and a time to give up;
A time to keep and a time to throw away;
A time to tear and a time to mend;
A time to be silent and a time to speak;
A time to love and a time to hate;
A time for war and a time peace.

Question

Who blesses your life and who makes you
laugh? Have you told your story? Have you
found the right time?

Chapter Seventeen

The Day of New Beginnings

I just spent an hour on the phone with a close friend. I couldn't tell him that I was writing or that I just didn't have time. I needed to take time with him. He needed to hear a voice that didn't judge and that cared about him as a person. He was struggling. He had recently attempted suicide and failed. I don't know much about depression. I have friends who struggle with it. A couple of them have been diagnosed with clinical depression, some with bipolar disorder.

I don't understand depression very well. I have read about it and it is confusing. I am not sure that even the scientists and doctors understand it very well. They just seem to treat symptoms. I do understand when my friends have mood swings and are on the low side of depression, even though I don't fully understand what they go through.

I remember back when my daughter was about three years old, I had a friend who was just a little bit older than I. She was a neighbor and was pregnant with her fifth child. She was normally a thin woman, rather pretty with shiny brown hair. She kept it long and she had a ready smile. She loved her kids and we often shared laughter and coffee in the mornings when our kids went down for a nap. I often saw her out playing in the sand box or stomping in mud puddles with her children and laughing with them. After her baby was born she was in the hospital for three days which wasn't unusual. She came home to four children and a husband.

All of us who were neighbors brought her meals so she wouldn't have to cook for the first few days and helped with the other children for a week or so to give her a chance to get on her feet again. But soon it was life as usual. Most of the women in our neighborhood worked or had kids of their own to tend to. I was her closest neighbor both physically and emotionally. We were good friends and shared a lot.

Perhaps two or three weeks after she came home with the new baby, I decided to resume our usual routine of sharing coffee and laughter. I knocked, hollered "It's just me!" and walked in as we both usually did. There was no answer but I could hear the baby crying desperately in the kitchen so I made my way there. My friend was standing holding the naked baby in one arm and stirring burning bacon with the other hand. She did not notice me as I took the baby from her and grabbed a towel from the counter. I shut off the stove. She continued to stir. I called her name over and over. She did not recognized that I was even there.

I called her husband at the place where he worked and asked him to come home. I bathed the baby and dressed him. He was not badly burned. He had a couple of splatter marks from the popping bacon.

When her husband came home he shook his head over and over. He said, "I thought she was going to be okay this time."

I asked him what he meant and he explained that after each birth his wife had gone into a depression. It was something the doctor called postpartum depression. This was the worst it had ever been. I told him to stop having babies.

I took the kids home with me while he took his wife to the doctor and when he came home it was without her. She was gone for quite awhile. I don't remember for sure how long, but I think it was close to three months. She was thin and tired looking when she came home, but it wasn't long before she was back to her old self and we were back to having our morning coffee. It was not without some pain however, as in those days some people thought of depression and mental illness as a curse and would not want to be associated with someone who had something like that. Some of the old neighbors stopped coming to help out or visit.

There are other types of depression besides the clinical or biological kinds. There are some that are related to environment and others that are related to past events.

I am a pretty upbeat kind of person. My glass is always at least half full so I wonder at people who get depressed about the way their life is playing out or the things that happen to them. I don't relate to the pessimist or the person who says, "If you don't expect good things to happen you won't be disappointed when they don't."

Don't get me wrong here. I have been down myself to the point of defeat at least a few times in my life. Probably the worst was when I discovered no matter what I said or how diligent and strong I was, I could not always protect my daughter from harm. I could not keep her wrapped up in a cocoon and out of harm's way. I felt so much like a failure I wanted to take my own life. .

There were two reasons for not ending my life. One was the fact that I still had a daughter to raise and the other was I knew it wasn't what God wanted me to do.   He had other plans for me.

Another time that I came close to suicide was when my heart was once again so broken by another failed marriage. My husband just did not need to be married anymore. That was what he said. I was sure I must have done something wrong and that I was worthless. There was no one in the world who would or could really love me. But wait, there was God. Yes He was there in my loneliness, too.

There were other times when I was at the low end of my existence but these two were the worst I think. I was either going to end it all or I was going to do something about it. What could I do? I was scraping bottom. I was tired of crying myself to sleep at night. I was having too many pity parties and that is not the fun kind of party. I had to learn about God's love for me first. I also had to learn to love myself.

The fact was, I was not depressed. I was knocked down and feeling sorry for myself. I was not happy but that isn't the same as depression. Depression is that unexplained mood that comes over a person and permeates their whole being. I have seen that mood arrive in others and have seen the struggle it sometimes takes to bring one's self out of it. Sometimes people just can't do that on their own. It takes a church. It takes a family. It takes someone who cares. It takes God and sometimes God sends in His A-team of professionals.

In my darkest hours, I called out to God and He heard me. Night after night as I cried myself to sleep, I called on Him and He comforted me. I found an inner strength that told me to get out of my own way and let God lift me up and carry me for a while.

In my darkest hours, I found a loving Father who really cares about me. No matter what my short comings or faults are, He is always still there. He won't interfere with any of us and our choices. He will stand behind us to catch us when we fall. He will pick us up.

I don't really know depression. The heaviness of it is not something I am familiar with. I do know God and His love is greater than all things. I know His grace to love and to heal. I know His strength and I am standing on His promise to never leave me.

I don't know why He wanted me to write about something I don't know much about. I do know that He will be there to pull you up. He did not give us a spirit of fear and of heaviness but one of light and joy.

Today is the day of new beginnings. Don't look back and stay in the past like Lot's wife or wish for changes and new things in the future. We do not know what the future will bring and wishing for it does not fill any of our present needs. Live for today, the day of new beginnings. God's grace is new every morning. God's love is always there.

If you are one of those being attacked by a spirit of depression, put on the full armor of God. Put on the helmet of salvation for the renewal of your mind. Strap on the sword of the spirit which is the word of God, the shield of faith and the breastplate of righteousness and gird your loins with the truth. Put on the shoes of peace. Stand on God's promise to protect you and to love you.   Don't worry or be upset. Let go and let God do it. He said He would and for sure He will. Let God hold you up and if you need it, let Him carry you for a while.

My heart goes out to those who suffer such things. I know the heart of God goes out to them too. Thinking about how much God loves us and what he has done for us fills my heart so full it overflows. When you are filled up like that you can't help but smile and it flows out into all you do. I hope that the love and joy flows right from the pages of this book and they lift you up and bring you peace. I wish you joy.

Prayer

Father God, give strength to those who need it and guidance and help to those who suffer such things as depression. Help me to be understanding and be more helpful to those in need.

Scripture

Philippians 4:4-7 (NAS)

Rejoice in the Lord always; again I say rejoice! Let your gentle spirit be known to all men. The Lord is near. Be anxious for nothing, but in everything by prayer and supplication with thanksgiving let your requests be made known to God. And all the peace of God, which surpasses all comprehension, will guard your hearts and your minds in Christ Jesus.

Questions

What makes you worried or depressed? Do you take your burdens to God?

SECTION TWO

STORIES FROM OTHERS WHO HAVE FOUND GOD IN THEIR OWN WAY AND IN DIFFERING PLACES

I truly appreciate these fine artists sending me their stories to use in the content of this book. It lets us know that we can all find God in amazing places if only we are willing to look.

Chapter Eighteen

Georgia On My Mind.

Story contributed by Georgia Yarbrough

It is Georgia Yarbrough's smile and her eyes that draw you to her. She has what I call a "God glow" about her that says "God lives here inside of me". Her love for others makes you want to be a recipient of one of her generous hugs.

I met Georgia at church. She is about five feet tall with her shoes on and seems to be a bundle of laid-back energy. It is as though she knows it never pays to hurry, that whatever she puts her mind to she will get done, all in God's timing.

She is so quiet that at first you think she is shy. She doesn't speak up very often but when she does, what she has to say is important.

Georgia helps out where ever and whenever she can. She volunteers at the food pantry, at the Day Café, cooking whenever there is a person or a family in need of food and any place else she feels God calls her to lend a hand. It wasn't always that way with her. Oh, I don't mean she wasn't generous or helpful. She probably has always been that type of person but by her own admission she has changed. Georgia found out that once you finally let God have a place in your life, things change in many ways.

Here is her story about finding God in everyday life in her own words.

I have believed in God since I was a child. As a young mother, I joined a church but it turned out to be not what I expected. I was attending often and learning a lot. I had young children and wanted to teach them about God. The church I went to was not receptive to children who were hyperactive or had any kind of issues. As a matter of fact, one of the authorities of the church called my husband Johnny and told him my son was not welcome there. That next time I was to leave him at home. My husband was furious. He said I was not ever to go back there and I didn't. It broke my heart and made me upset. I stopped going to church altogether but I never stopped believing in God.

Eventually my kids grew up and got families of their own. Johnny passed away in 2007. Johnny had not been easy to live with sometimes but I loved him and I missed him terribly. I continued to grieve and went into a depression that lasted about two years. I stayed home most of the time and often found myself crying for no reason. I got so I did not even want to go out of the house.

My neighbor Esther invited me to volunteer at the food pantry where she worked. One day I decided it was time to quit feeling sorry for myself and get out and do something so I joined her.

I was shy at first but could feel the need of these people. It felt good to help someone else for a change. I met a lot of really nice people. I learned I could help make people feel better just by being there and listening to them.

Still something was missing. Esther invited me to attend church with her and her husband Phil. It took a while but I finally did go with them.

The moment I walked into the church, I knew I had found a home. Everyone was so friendly and inviting. I started going to church on a regular basis. I was always welcomed with open arms.

I eventually joined a Bible study group led by the pastor. There I made friends with other people on a closer level. Then I took the membership class that the pastor offered. Since that time, I have joined a small group Bible study and a prayer group. I have helped with the children and have helped develop a retreat for women.

I still work at the food pantry. Often people just need someone who cares. They gravitate towards me for some reason. I just take their hands and listen. Often I pray with them if they are receptive to that.

I found a home at the church and with the people who attend there. I hope I pass God on with the things I do to help others. I am being led to talk about the scripture that says "Do unto others as you would have them do unto you." Luke 6:31 The Pastor asked me to share that and my testimony with the congregation.

I woke up in the middle of the night and just couldn't get back to sleep. These thoughts just kept going around in my head. I got up and wrote them all down. When I shared the story and the "Do unto others..." scripture, I decided I would just read it. I was so scared. So, I started to read it but kept losing my place on the paper so I just gave up and told it. I know I didn't say everything that I had planned to say. I guess it doesn't matter. What matters is that I got to share what God wanted me to say.

Georgia found God in the neighbor who invited her to help at the food pantry, in the Bible study group, in the people who attended the church she went to and finally in the help she could give those in need.

Georgia touched everyone's life the day she first gave her testimony, and she has gone on to tell her story in other places. She continues to find God in many places so her testimony continues.

Prayer

"Father help me to be like Georgia who continues to find ways to share your story with others."

Scripture

Luke 6:31 (NAS)

Do to others what you would have them do to you.

Luke 6:36 (NAS)

Be merciful just as your Father is merciful.

Question

What are you sharing today?

Chapter Nineteen

Differing Views

Story contributed by Libby Franck

I was taking a sabbatical to work on this book and staying with my friend Anne-Marie Forer. We both decided we needed a break and what better way than to have dinner with friends. So we picked up Libby Franck and took her out to dinner. She asked what I had been doing. I told her about this book and that I was doing a writing retreat to work on it. I told her the book is about finding God in everyday places and diverse situations. Our conversation went on to other things, but Libby brought it back to the book and told me this story.

Last Sunday I was on my way to a musical concert at a friend's house. I was early so I walked to the end of the street and sat on a cemetery wall in the autumn sunshine to memorize a poem. A woman strolled down the road. "Out for a walk too?" she said. "Yes," I replied. "I am working on a program we are doing here in this cemetery. We are telling the stories of some of the historical people who are buried here. It will be next weekend."

"You shouldn't be doing that," she said in a judgmental tone. "You don't know if they are in heaven or hell. Don't do that program."

I pointed out that we were enhancing the knowledge of the town's history. And no one was forced to come if they didn't want to.

She went on about how sacrilegious that was. I said we didn't mean to be disrespectful. This was a way of educating those interested in history.

*She went on and on. I said I was leaving, going off to listen to some music. "Where?" she said. "In a **private** home!" I replied walking down the road.*

The next day at CVS the woman at the checkout counter said, "Yesterday everybody was just in the worst mood. Don't know why. I was praying hard. Then some nuns came in and I asked them to pray with me. Our personal prayers together made it a much better day."

"I like that." I replied. And left the store with a smile.

I like Libby's story. It is a simple story but to me it is a story about attitude. It is really hard to see God in an attitude of judgement and condemnation. It is not up to us to know whether a person is in heaven or hell. It isn't up to us to tell others what they should and shouldn't do unless of course they are doing something that will hurt themselves and others.

We don't know if the first person Libby meets is a Christian or not, but we do know she was condemning and judgmental and needed an attitude adjustment. We don't know much about the second person either but we do know she was a praying woman. She made Libby smile and she made me smile too.

Prayer

"Father help me to be the kind of person who leaves people with a smile and help me to recognize my judgmental attitude. Whenever I find myself doing that help me to take it to you and ask you to rid me of it."

Scripture

Philippians 4:4-5 (NAS)

Rejoice in the Lord, again I say rejoice! Let your gentle spirit be known to all men.

Question

What about you? Are you making people smile with your attitude today?

Do you need an attitude adjustment?

Chapter Twenty

Finding God Through Grief

Story contributed by Lorna McDonald Czarnota

God isn't only in the easy times or the beauty of our lives. I have found Him in places many people would never have gone. You can find Him in the sunrise and sunset, but you can also find Him in your tears. My friend Lorna MacDonald Czarnota says she is not sure she found God in her grief but she knows He found her through it. Here is her story.

Grief is such a personal experience. We all travel through it sometime, and it's not just about losing a living being. We grieve lost jobs, lost opportunities, lost homes and friendships. People go through the stages of grief at their own pace and in any order. The stages of grief were identified by Kulber and Ross as denial, anger, bargaining, depression and acceptance. Psychologically speaking, once we navigate through these stages, we are able to move on in our own lives as whole individuals. This is the science of grieving but what about the spiritual side of the journey? Do we ever really stop grieving? Will we ever feel whole when we have lost something that seemed such a part of our identity? Maybe the answer is in the identity piece.

I identify myself as a Christian. This means I believe in one God and that Jesus Christ is one third of that Godhead. That Jesus, as the human side of God gave up his life so I could live forever with God. But is this belief enough to overcome grief? I don't think so. I don't think it is enough to say nothing but God matters or that if you've lost someone you know they will still live on eternally or even to believe that someday you will see them again. More is needed in the moment of pain. Being human and loving means fear, doubt, pain and all the other emotions we have.

I lost my father on the heels of burying my very old dog, my first dog, and two months later, my mother. Both of these passings had been expected and every time I left my dog or my mom, I said goodbye as if it was the last time, because it could have been. But when my dad got sick, it was like someone had sucked all the breath out of me. How could he have gotten so sick, so suddenly? He'd never been sick but once in the time he was my dad. Of course, that once had been big—he had cancer, but he had overcome it. Now I watched my big strong daddy languish in the hospital. There were a couple times of hope but he kept bouncing back into the ICU. After a while, they kept him sedated. He got to point where communicating wasn't possible. I still have his notepad—the one where he wrote to us because he had a tracheal tube, and his messages went from neat and coherent to a slur to just a wiggly line that disappeared off the page. It broke my heart and still does, even as I write this. He was my teacher. He was the one I could talk to for hours. Now, there was nothing. Oh, and I had breast cancer, which was the easy part. Arguments and hard feelings spread in the family and I had only my significant other to lean on. Daddy couldn't help me deal with anything the way he always did. Daddy was dying.

I cannot honestly say that I took it to God, though I'm sure I prayed. I know I never felt angry at Him. I might have asked, "Why?" I may have asked for strength. Some things from that "really, terrible, horrible, awful year" are a blur. I say I must have prayed because I was raised to believe in God and have always, since a child, believed that I have an angel. Even so, it didn't change the situation or my sorrow. As I write, it's been seven years since Dad passed but I still cry hopelessly at anything that reminds me of him. I still wonder if signing permission to have him removed from life support was right. I still look back in disdain at the hospital, believing they gave him poor care. But I never blamed God for any of it. People do, you know. They say, "If there is a God, and he's so loving, why did he make or let this happen?" I never did and never will blame God.

Our death in this world is because we broke the rules. You know, the "original sin" when Adam and Eve ate of the Fruit of Knowledge. Parents are always telling their children not to do harmful things, and children do disobey. Maybe knowing this kept me from blaming God that and the knowledge that he sent Jesus to erase that original sin. God is our Heavenly Father, who wants only the best for us. He is our constant friend and when all others fail—when family fails—He always remains beside us.

I didn't find God in my grief—God found me!

When doctors in Dad's hometown hospital finally said they could do no more for him and he was so incoherent that he couldn't make decisions for himself, I ordered him brought to where I live and a better hospital.

My sister and her husband, myself and my partner had arrived at the hospital that morning to see Dad. He had just had the two most productive days in the seven weeks he had been in the hospital, so moving him had been smart. They had equipment to get him out of bed and into a chair for the first time. He had smiled at the nurses. The surgeon was ready to wean him off the ventilator. But as I pulled up to the hospital, my cell phone rang. It was the lead doctor. "His heart is failing. You need to be here." I look back now and see the miracle that we had arrived before it was too late. I had just had my cancer surgery two days prior or maybe I would not have been able to be there.

We all sat down with the doctor who explained that they didn't know what had caused the swelling in my dad's throat in the first place, and now his organs were shutting down. He told us that the only option for us at that time was to let them put Dad in a coma until they could figure out what to do and then they could not guarantee he would ever be the same. In other words, my vibrant dad might be a vegetable. This is why Dad had a DNR and made me his health proxy. He didn't consider that state as living. The doctors had to resuscitate and soon, so my sister and I had talked. We made the most difficult decision of our lives. It was best to let him go.

We stood on either side of Dad's bed, holding his hands. He was pale and unmoving. The nurses were so gentle and amazing. "It's time." they said. And we both told Dad how much we loved him. The nurses disconnected the life-support. But Dad kept breathing! I knew in an instant why. He wanted to be sure we were okay. I said, "Dad, it's okay. We're going to be okay. Mom is waiting for you." That's when he died. I wasn't really sure we would be okay. My sister and I were at odds with each other. But I look back now and I think I actually saw my mother holding out her hand for him. And, what happened next is truly one of those things one cannot explain.

The nurse asked if we needed anything. Without thinking, I said, "We need a minister. Is there someone here who can come pray with us?" She said she would check and moments later returned to say the only clergy in the building that day was a Catholic priest, did we mind. I didn't mind. I felt we needed God's comfort, especially since my sister was now hyperventilating. God works in mysterious ways, that's what they say, and I've seen it too much in my life to deny the fact. Everybody knew my dad, and his claim to local fame was his ability to tell a good joke. I absolutely believe, in my deepest heart of hearts, that what happened was God let Dad come back for one last joke.

The nurse sent for the priest, and he arrived very quickly. When he entered the room, I suppose we all stood rather uncertain, or maybe expectant. Not being Catholic, we thought he would say a nice prayer of comfort. But instead, without any word to us, he circled Dad's bed sprinkling him with holy water and speaking Latin. I think it was Latin, but you see, the Catholic priest was from Pakistan and we could not understand his English let alone his Latin. A Pakistani Catholic priest giving last rites in Latin to a Lutheran man was hysterical to us. Our grief was broken by the four of us, especially my sister and I breaking out into laughter that made us hiccup and gave us pains in our sides. One moment we were sobbing, the next we were laughing with Dad. No offense intended to my Catholic friends, but I think you can imagine this. Ever since that day, I have believed that God actually has a great sense of humor, and I've had a different kind of relationship with him.

It's not so much that I found God in my grief, but that I finally saw God—the real Him--the loving and like me Him. When I talk to Him we have real conversations. A lot like the ones I used to have with Dad. And, I talk to Dad too, because I think God left the door open a crack so we can do that.

We will, all people, travel the road of grief, large and small, and do it in our own way and time, but with God as a friend and guide, the road will be less bumpy. Beyond the darkness, there is light. Beyond the sorrow—there is laughter.

Prayer

"Father help us in our times of grief and help us to see the way to comfort those who suffer

silently in these times. Whether it be from loss of a loved one or some other devastating loss."

Scripture

Galatians 6:2 (NAS)

Bear one another's burdens and thereby fulfill the law of Christ.

Question

Have you suffered loss? How can you help someone who is going through that?

Chapter Twenty One

IT'S A HEALING HAPPENING

Story contributed by Nina Scarlet

When Nina Scarlett said she would send me a story for this book I was thrilled. She is a gifted artist and talented speaker. She has had many physical problems over the years and has experienced healing in a way most of us do not. She has a deep love for God and His people. Below is just one of her stories.

Healings, or as I have come to call them, miracles, often happen in some of the most unexpected places at the most unexpected times. I've had many healings of many different kinds. The one I want to share with you now is not what most of my friends and family would consider the most crucial or amazing but for me it was stunning. Yup, I was absolutely, positively stunned!

It occurred during a prison bible study. There were four of us from the church - the Pastor, myself and the parents of one of the inmates. The inmates were a mix of men and women, which could be the very reason some of them came to the study, a chance to be with the opposite sex. We had a very captive audience for our purposes, which was to bring the love of Christ to each one who came to the study.

One night the Pastor was showing a very short video about a father and his son. Now I cannot remember the entire content of that particular video but what I can remember is God reaching out His hand to my heart, my very broken heart and hearing the words, "I don't care what anyone has told you Nina, you are my child.   I planned your life from the very time of your conception, I love you and I am your Heavenly Father, the Father who wanted you to be born. And YES, Nina, your deepest desire will one day happen. When we meet in Heaven you will dance bare-footed endlessly with me to the song Daddy's Little Girl because YOU ARE MY LITTLE GIRL, Abba Father."

Now if you had asked me at the very moment if I was still hurting because of events that took place between my father and I, I would have told you absolutely not. My Dad and I had talked things through and as far as I was concerned we had rectified our past. What I neglected to recognize is what most of us don't see, the deep, huge scar all of it left on my heart, the unwanted child's heart. Oh, how wonderful it is to know that my life was no accident. I had and HAVE purpose. God chose me and LOVES me. He also loves you. Go ahead take a walk, take a run, have a sit down or a kneel down, whatever works best for you. Just take the time right now and ask Him to be your Father. Ask to be accepted into His family and recognize the fact that you are His child. You're gonna love His answer!

Nina's story touched a spot in my heart and I imagine it did yours too. Jesus too, must have felt what it was like to be the unwanted child when He cried from the cross, "My God, my God why have you forsaken me?" He went through all that and more so that we can say, "Abba Father."

When I had cancer, I expected God to heal me and He did. When I was in a car accident and couldn't walk for three months, I knew God was there encouraging me to get up and start walking and I did. God doesn't always do what we ask and sometimes the healing we pray for just doesn't come. God knows what plans He has for us and what is best for us. We do not know what His plans are, but we do know we have a heavenly Father who loves us in spite of ourselves. He loves us unconditionally and will be there with us and will not forsake us or leave us to go through this life alone.

Prayer

"Father we ask forgiveness for our doubt and thank you for giving the gift of your Son so that we too can be adopted into your family and call you Father Abba."

Scripture

2 Corinthians 13:11 (NAS)

Finally, brethren, rejoice, be made complete, be comforted, be like-minded, live in peace; and the God of love and peace will be with you.

Question

What healing have you experienced? Do you know someone who has experienced unexplained physical or mental healing?

Chapter Twenty-two

Bananas and Crackers

Story contributed by Cora Jo Ciampi

I was delighted when Cora Jo Ciampi agreed to contribute a story for this book. I know a lot of her stories and that is because she is a sister. Not just any sister either. She is my baby sister. The youngest girl in the family. She is a talented author and has a great sense of humor. I can remember some of the things we did together when she was a young mother and most of them make me smile or laugh. I know you will relate to this story.

In all the work you are doing, work the best you can. Work as if you were doing it for the Lord, not for people. Colossians 3:25

Baby in the grocery cart reaching for anything within reach as I write down the price of each item I put into the basket of the cart. The amount on the little notebook is adding up fast. I have $20.00. My precious baby boy eats things now besides formula. Bananas, rice cereal, applesauce. I needed to feed his father and myself as well. A can of tuna, the cheaper box of mac n' cheese, some canned corn and green beans go into the cart. Baby food in little jars with a healthy, happy looking baby on the label *go into the basket. Why does such a small jar cost so much?*

By the time I reached the fresh vegetables and fruit my little notebook revealed that I was very close to my limit. Don't forget taxes! I picked out three bananas and looked longingly at the fresh corn, fresh green beans and strawberries. My mind went home to Mom's garden. I could surely get "fresh" there. But no, I'm on my own now, grown up, married with a baby.

There was that baby in the cart starting to fuss in earnest now. My constant companion for the next 18 years wanted to touch, taste, feel everything and anything. I took the colorful sticker off a banana and put it on his finger. He laughed as he tried to get the sticker off his fingers. I picked another sticker off a banana and stuck it to his forehead. He felt the sticker and laughed. By now we are in the dreaded check-out lane. What if I added wrong on my little notebook? What if I didn't have enough money?

My restless baby was no longer happy with the little sticker on his forehead so like a good mommy I helped him. When you take a Band-Aid off, you pull it fast and it doesn't hurt so much. I pulled the sticker off his forehead. He screamed, little red dots of blood came to the surface in a perfect circle where the sticker had been. I was horrified! So was the well-dressed older woman in the line behind me.

"I cannot believe you just did that to your poor child! Look at him, he's bleeding!"

I am not sure how I got out of the store. I don't know if I had enough money to pay for the things in my cart. All I knew was she couldn't believe I was such a horrible mommy!

Later that week I walked over to visit my aunt who was helping me make little shorts for my baby boy. She had seven children. She saw the red little circle on his forehead and asked if he had fallen down. I burst into tears and told her the whole awful story. Bless my aunt, she laughed, patted my arm and said that woman probably didn't have children and if she did someone else took care of them. My aunt put a Band-Aid on my wound.

Fly down the path of my life. Fly past many, many failures and successes in raising three babies. Zoom in a grocery store with me in a hurry. I don't like grocery shopping. I just want to get what I need and get home. It seems as though everyone in town is in the same boat. The aisles are crowded and slow.

I turn into one of the aisles I need and there taking up most of the space is a young woman with one of the carts with the big seats in the front for at least two children. There are, in fact, two little ones in those seats and another older child hanging on the front of the cart. She seems to be deliberating over her next choice. I am sure she heard me sigh as I wheeled my cart around and headed in the opposite direction.

Down the next aisle, I dodged and maneuvered around a man on an electric cart. In the following aisle I am reaching for the oatmeal when I hear a scream at the other end of the aisle.   There she is. The child on the front of the cart is hopping up and down, crying hard and holding his foot. She apparently had run over his toe. The other two children in the seats have broken in to a box of crackers and are eating them and dropping them at an alarming rate. That self-same sigh was about to escape my mouth again when I saw she had a calculator in her hand. I saw her trying to comfort her boy, I saw--- wait--- I saw a young mom put a banana sticker on the forehead of her baby. I saw her rip it off. I heard the older woman condemn her. The Band-Aid my aunt had put on my wound ripped off and I bled all over again.

"Oh boy" I said to the more modern mom. "Here let me help with your cart while you fix the toe."

She looked at me as if I were from outer space. "What?" she said ready for a barrage of condemnation.

125

"Hey you two!" I said to the little culprits in the seats. "Can I have a cracker?"

They laughed and I ate wet, soggy crackers while she consoled the poor toe. No band-aid here. Maybe instead she would see a glimpse of Christ Jesus here. I know I was.

"Thanks," she said as she got herself and her constant companions in order and headed down the aisle.

"It's what we do," I said. "It's what we do."

I can so relate to this story. There are so many times when we wish we could just get on with it and all the noise and distraction would disappear. You so often remember the times when you are condemned by others. You live with it. Sometimes you believe it. You don't have to. You just have to know what it is that God thinks of you. You are adopted into His family and as a child of the King, you reign with Him. You are blessed and loved and precious in His sight.

Prayer

Father God let us see others as you see them. Let us not harm but do good to all those in our keeping and those who cross our paths. Let us

bless them and let your light of love shine through us.

Scripture

1 John 3:18 (NAS)

My little children, let us not love in word or in tongue, but in deed and in truth. And by this, we know that we are of the truth, and shall assure our hearts before Him.

Question

When it is so easy to find the fault in others, do you instead try catch someone doing good?

Chapter Twenty Three

A Man Named Peter

Story Contributed Dr. Michael Lockett.

Mike Lockett and I became friends through storytelling. We met at the national festival in Jonesborough, Tennessee and have been friends since that first meeting. We work together on many things. Mike has been doing storytelling in Taiwan for many years and now is also travelling to China as a storyteller. He has written and translated children's books in both Chinese and Spanish. Here is a story about Taiwanese man he met in China.

"I have a new name. My name is Peter." These excited words were part of a conversation in China that still warms my heart.

I sat in an upper room above a restaurant waiting for dinner with friends. We had arrived early for what was going to be a private gathering of Taiwanese businessmen who lived in China. A growing number of Chinese men have left Taiwan to seek out economic opportunities in China. Some have opened restaurants. One man I met runs a security business. One is a builder, another is an investor and another sells books. The rest have a variety of positions with one thing in common. They all are good family men who live separate from their families back in Taiwan. These men came together during the course of doing business. They do business with each other to support one another in their efforts to succeed in a new land. They spend time together when not working to fill the void that comes from living apart from their wives and their children. Common activities include dining together, going fishing, hitting golf balls together at a golfing range and even just having tea together.

How do I know about these men and their activities? I have been among them multiple times as I travel from Taiwan to China to give storytelling programs. "Tell me more about your programs. Tell me more about the children." These are common statements they make to me. This circle of friends seems happy to include me in their get-togethers. I, in turn, very much enjoy their company. We share an exchange of cultures whenever I am fortunate enough to enjoy being among them as they gather to socialize.

It was one of these evenings when I met a man I had not seen at one of the get-togethers. In my limited Chinese I said, "Hello, what is your name?" He shook his head "no" and looked away.

"Did I say it wrong?" I asked my friend, Tony. "I tried to ask him what his name was."

"You said it properly," said Tony. Then he talked for a moment in Chinese to his friend. The friend responded back and looked sheepish.

"He does not have an English name and feels embarrassed," Tony told me.

"Please tell him he does not need to be embarrassed. I know a lot of people have English names in addition to their Chinese names. But, you don't have to have one." But before Tony could translate these words to his Chinese counterpart, the friend added something else.

Tony said, "You give him a name. He wants you to give him an English name."

The conversation that follows was a three-way talk – back and forth from English to Chinese and Chinese back to English.

"A name is something special that each person should choose by themselves," I suggested.

"I want you to give me a name," persisted the individual.

This is when I asked, "What do you like to do in your free time."

He answered, "I really like to fish."

That is when it hit me – "PETER" – the great fisherman – the disciple of Christ. "There once was a fisherman, I told him... an ordinary man named Simon who had to work very hard to make a living by fishing in the Sea of Galilea in Israel. This man was chosen as a disciple by Jesus." Then I told him through my friend about Jesus Christ and how Simon followed Jesus and learned from him. I told him how Jesus called Simon "A Fisher of Men" and how Jesus later said, "Your name will be PETER. You will be the ROCK on which my church will be built."

"I like that name. My English name will be PETER. It is a good name, a strong name." Then it became time to leave the upper room and walk downstairs for the dinner with the entire group of friends. As we reached the main floor, another member of the group of Taiwanese businessmen entered the room. "I have a new name," said Peter in Chinese. "Wo jou Peter. My name is Peter."

The new man who entered the conversation had accepted Jesus Christ as his personal savior a few years earlier in Taiwan. He spoke in English to me to find out what had just transpired then begged to speak alone to Peter. The two sat at the far end of the table and talked rapidly in Chinese for almost an hour while I and the rest of the group dined and talked together on any number of topics. Then I saw the two men walking towards me. "Peter wants to thank you for giving him a name. He and I will be talking a lot more. He wants to learn more about Jesus and the things he taught his disciples. He wants to accept Jesus as his savior."

The two men walked back to the far end of the room to continue their conversation. I have not seen either man since. Yet I still think of that evening often. I feel that God worked through me to bring His word to a listener who was waiting to hear words of healing and love that he needed. How fitting that God worked through me to bring his grace to a new saved soul, a man called "PETER."

It is fitting that this be the final chapter for this book. The Bible tells us a story about a man named Peter and how he climbed out of the boat and walked on the water to get to Jesus. He didn't start to sink until he started to doubt his own ability instead of relying on Jesus to get him there. He began to sink when he took his eyes off of Jesus.

I have said many times "You can't walk on water if you never get out of the boat". It seems to me that Mike got out of the boat when he talked with this man and gave him a new name.

How often we wish we had said just the right thing at the right time. How often we wish we had gotten out of the boat and not worried about what others would think of what we were saying or doing. How often we don't say or do something because we doubt ourselves and don't rely on Christ Jesus to lift us up and see us through to the end.

Prayer

Father God, Thank you for giving us a new name and a new nature through Christ Jesus our redeemer. Thank you for giving us the strength to step out of the boat and step up to tell the story.

Scripture

Matthew 14:25-31 (NAS)

Shortly before dawn Jesus went out to them, walking on the water. When the disciples saw him walking on the lake they were terrified. "It's a ghost," they said and cried out in fear.

But Jesus immediately said to them "Take courage, It is I, don't be afraid."

"Lord, if it is you" Peter replied "tell me to come to you on the water."

"Come" he said.

Then Peter got down out of the boat and walked on the water and came toward Jesus but when he saw the wind, he was afraid and beginning to sink he cried "Lord, save me."

Immediately Jesus reached out his hand and caught him and lifted him up. "You of little faith" he said "Why did you doubt?"

And when they climbed into the boat the wind died down.

Question

How many times have you been afraid to get out of the boat? How many times have you missed the miracle because you were afraid to walk on water?

Georgia Yarbrough from Tilton, NH volunteers at the food pantry, at the Day Café, cooking whenever there is a person or a family in need of food and any place else she feels God calls her to lend a hand. She lives with her sister in the house her parents owned when she was growing up.

Libby Franck is a gifted storyteller who performs historical interpretations of people like Sarah Jessica Hale, Betsy Ross and Edna Dean Proctor. She does extensive research on the stories she writes and tells to get them as historically accurate as possible.

Lorna McDonald Czarnota is an award winning storyteller and author. She holds a Masters in special education and is certified in trauma counseling. She is highly regarded for her work with at risk youth and their teachers and parents.

Nina Scarlet has an amazing artistic talent. She is a talented painter and she is a gifted speaker and leader. She has devoted much of her life to bringing God's light to a very dark world. She has a special talent to relate to children of all ages.

Cora Jo Ciampi is an author, storyteller, teacher and librarian. She has told stories in many locations across the US. She won the award for Children's Librarian of the year and continues to share traditional folk tales as well as stories of her own creation.

Dr. Michael Lockett is a retired school teacher, author, musician and storyteller who shares story, music and culture with many children across the globe. His books have been translated into many languages including Chinese. He travels often to Taiwan and China where he delights audiences of all ages.

AFTERWORD

Sitting in this rocking chair beside the fireplace, watching as those light pink fingers reach out to pull the sun up into the sky and give the earth its morning light, I am amazed. I realize that I have found God in ordinary places, in some very amazing animals and in many human beings.

I asked a friend the other day "How do you see God?"

She said, "I find the whole of creation to be amazing. Only God could have created such a complexity of nature and humanity."

I feel the same way. Only a loving God would have created such a place for us to live and learn to love. We are here to learn to love. He provides for us and cares for us as only a Father would. Only a Father who loves us so much could give His Son to die for us so we can call Him Father.

It was only three days since the arrest and crucifixion of Jesus when Cleopas and another of the disciples were walking home from Jerusalem to Emmaus. He joined them on the road. They were distraught and disappointed and were discussing what had taken place in Jerusalem the last three days. He asked what they were discussing and

Cleopas said "Are you the only one in all of the country who has not heard?" and began to tell Jesus all that had happened. They were so wrapped up in their sorrow and disappointment that they could not see Him.

Then He taught them all the scriptures concerning Himself and His journey on Earth. When they arrived at Cleopas' house, they invited Him in to eat and stay the night. Cleopas was just not ready to let this man go.

When they sat down to eat Jesus took the bread and blessed it and broke it and began to pass it to them. That is when they recognized Him. Was it the act of breaking the bread and blessing it or did they suddenly see the scars on His wrists? How did they come out of their sadness and open their eyes to see Jesus? What did they see?

I think they saw the face of Christ and the love that He had for them. The love He has for us this day. The love of a Christ who died for us and was resurrected to save us and give us eternal life with His Father. The Christ who even just three days after He suffered such a horrible death and had just come out of the tomb, loved them so much He took time to walk with them seven miles. The one who taught them the prophesies about Himself and the one who saved them and brought them home again.

In this book I have shared some of the ways I see Him in everyday life and some of the unusual places I have found Him. Others have shared their own stories too.

It is my privilege as an adopted child to crawl up on His lap and say "Aba, Father."

It is my responsibility to care for what He has so generously given to me.

It is my honor to worship Him, to praise His holy name and to love Him because He first loved me.

Thanks go to all who have contributed to this adventure and have so generously shared their story and their lives with us.

How do you see Him? What stories can you share about when and where you found Him?

Made in the USA
Middletown, DE
08 February 2022